MW01170465

THE FUNDAMENTAL 5
REVISITED

EXCEPTIONAL INSTRUCTION IN EVERY SETTING

Sean Cain and Mike Laird

Sherilynn Cotten and Jayne Ellspermann

Copyright © 2021 Sean Cain, Mike Laird,
Sherilynn Cotten, Jayne Ellspermann

All rights reserved.

ISBN: 9798477693238

DEDICATION

This book is dedicated to every teacher that welcomed us into their classroom while they were doing the most important job of all—teaching students. Everything we know about effective instruction we learned because we were afforded the opportunity to watch you work.

CONTENTS

ACKNOWLEDGMENTS

The authors would like to acknowledge the educators and teammates that have been instrumental in our continuous pursuit of exceptional teaching, enhanced student opportunities, excellent schools, and the development of this book.

Robert Brezina, E. Don Brown, Lesa Cain, Don Cotten, James Davis, Barbara Fine, Jo Hoeppner, David Martinez, Leslie Meek, Harry Miller, Jeanette Nelson, Andrea Payne, Gwen Poteet, Traci Tousant, Tricia Tsang

1 INTRODUCTION

The Basic Practices of Quality Instruction Are Not a Secret

When Sean Cain and Mike Laird wrote the above statement in 2010, they knew it was TRUE. In 2021, the authors (Cain, Laird, Cotten, and Ellspermann) now know that sentence is only PARTIALLY TRUE. Yes, the profession can point to a body of practice that is considered "High-Yield." The written identification of similarities and differences, student to student collaboration, non-linguistic representation, and goal setting are just a few examples of these practices. However, for too many field-based members of the profession, the knowledge of these and other high-yield practices remains cursory. As a profession, we confuse knowledge with implementation. We then confuse implementation with expertise. We also confuse the random occurrence of personal preference with the high frequency, high quality implementation of a cohesive and integrated package of exceedingly effective practices. The impetus of our work is to assist teachers as they progress through the stages of knowledge, implementation, and expertise, making their work more impactful and significantly enhancing the academic performance of their students.

From the early 2000s up to March 2020, the authors spent the bulk of their professional work helping teachers implement better practice. They believe if a teacher is going to break a sweat working (which all teachers do), that work should produce the greatest possible student outcome (which it rarely does). In essentially all of the 250,000+ classrooms the authors have observed in their careers, some student performance is left on the table. As long-time educators and practitioners, we respect teachers too much to let them squander their effort by engaging in lesser practices, regardless of the cause or reason, be it a lack of knowledge or understanding, underlying habits and routines, or by deliberate design.

With full transparency, in our endeavor to significantly increase the effectiveness of the typical teacher, we have not been 100% successful. Yes, tens of thousands of teachers have improved the overall quality of their daily instruction based on either reading **The Fundamental 5** and/or receiving training and support to implement those practices. Even more teachers have read **The Fundamental 5** text or heard **The Fundamental 5** talk and have done little to consciously improve their craft. This is stated without recrimination. In fact, there is some logic to the decision of those who have selected not to engage. Frankly, in many settings there has not been a compelling need. This is not to suggest that in some settings teachers were already 100% effective and outcomes for all students were already optimized. If such a setting exists, the authors have not stumbled across it in their years of crisscrossing the country. It is the understanding that, in some settings, the performance of more than enough students is deemed to be adequate. As such, there is little external, organizational, and/or personal motivation to improve pedagogy. In these cases, **The Fundamental 5** has been judged to be interesting (true), but not required (disappointing).

In March 2020, the education environment, along with almost everything else on the planet, changed. In August 2021, the education environment changed again.

As schools and classrooms transition from pandemic to post-pandemic operations, the high frequency, high quality implementation of better instructional practice is no longer a professional suggestion; it is a requisite of professional duty. Essentially all students have had their education impacted negatively by the pandemic. Some students less negatively than others, but all have been impacted. This means that going forward from August 2021, in addition to making expected levels of academic progress in current year content (already a difficult task), teachers also must address COVID-19 deficits of varying severity (a new and even more difficult task).

To demonstrate how daunting this task truly is, consider Figure 1.1. On this graph, the vertical axis represents student knowledge and achievement. The horizontal axis represents the grade level of the student. The line represents the growth in student knowledge from the first day of kindergarten through graduation. Essentially, students enter school in kindergarten with little academic knowledge and skills, attend school for thirteen years, and then graduate possessing a considerable level of academic knowledge and skills. This was an impressive and consistent feat that was accomplished year after year, from 2001 to 2020.

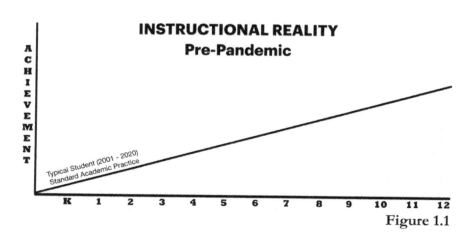

Figure 1.1

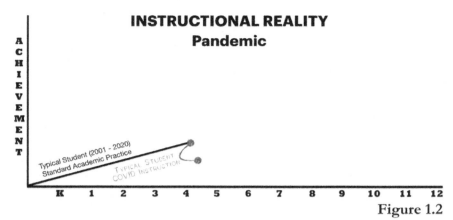

Figure 1.2

In March of 2020, this changed. From March 2020 thru August 2021, the system that produced the predictable, incremental growth in student academic knowledge and skills was disrupted. During those seventeen months, there was not steady growth in student knowledge and skills. Progress was inconsistent, a *1-step forward, 2-steps back* dance to an unsteady beat. During this time, the line of student performance shifted down...everywhere, for everyone. This was no one's fault. Not school systems, school administrators, teachers, students, nor parents—no one. Evidently, this is what happens in a pandemic (Figure 1.2).

As schools emerge from the pandemic, there is a natural desire and professional pressure to "get back to normal." This is understandable. However, a sprint to "normal" creates a significant

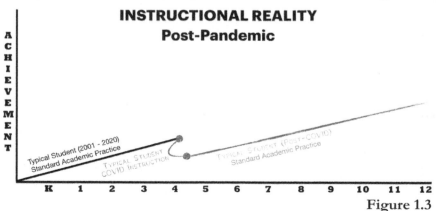

Figure 1.3

problem. If schools and teachers sprint back to "normal," a predictable trend line of academic growth will return. However, as Figure 1.3 shows, because schools are re-starting normal operations at a lower starting point, the student growth line produced by pre-pandemic (i.e., "normal") instructional practices and processes will now produce a lower student outcome. Again, this is no one's fault. This is simply a result of a mismatch between starting points of the old normal and the new normal.

The gap between the new, post-pandemic student growth line and the now non-existent, pre-pandemic student growth line represents the persistent COVID-19 gap that students are carrying forward. Simply put, if instructional practices and processes do not significantly improve, then students currently in our schools will face diminished educational outcomes when compared to their peers who graduated prior to or during the pandemic (Figure 1.4). There is no fault to be assigned for the cause of this COVID-19 gap. However, educators have a professional duty to address it. A sprint back to "normal" is not a responsible option.

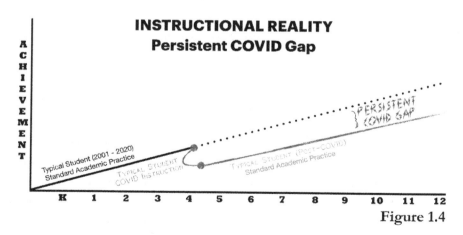

Figure 1.4

Going forward, better instructional practices are no longer a suggestion. The increase in both frequency and quality of high-yield instructional practices, in every classroom, by every teacher, must become the post-pandemic reality. Couple that paradigm-altering fact with the fact that we have a better understanding of the five fundamental instructional practices and hard earned knowledge on how to best adopt and implement **The Fundamental 5** as default instructional practice. Our belief is that an updated version of **The Fundamental 5** is a vital resource for today's teachers. **The Fundamental 5** is now more important than ever.

A Quick History Lesson: A Perfect Storm

The Fundamental 5 was not invented. **The Fundamental 5** was always there. It is a pattern of practice that was *identified* by a team of practitioners. The discovery of this pattern was the result of an educational perfect storm. In the late 1990s, the professional literature identifying, quantifying, and describing better instructional practices became more widely available. In this same time frame, states began to adopt rudimentary accountability standards. This was the operating environment in which the authors were transitioning from teachers to campus administrators. With this transition, came the mandate from their respective districts, *"Meet state standards…or else."*

The authors had internal and external motivations to ensure that their students, teachers, and campuses were successful. They were fortunate to have a better road map for accomplishing this than the campus administrators they succeeded. This story would have ended there if not for one more fortuitous event. In 2004, Dr. Shirley Neeley was named the Texas Commissioner of Education. Previously a successful and popular school superintendent, she was tasked with the unenviable job of administering state mandated sanctions against "low performing" schools and school districts. Dr. Neeley understood struggling schools did not struggle due to a lack of educator care and/or effort. She believed, and the authors concur, that the vast majority of struggling schools do so due to a lack of resources, support, and/or direction. With this belief and the resources at her disposal, she created an office of Innovative School

Redesign. The office, eventually comprised of three successful former principals, was given access to every public school campus in the state of Texas and the ability to travel to any school of note, anywhere in the country. Additionally, the team was provided an adequate travel budget to make this possible. The mandate of the Innovative School Redesign team: do everything in their power to make sure the Commissioner does NOT have to sanction a campus. Where the Texas Legislature's intent was to create a bigger stick to motivate struggling schools to improve, Dr. Neeley's intent was to build a safety net to give struggling schools a fighting chance to be successful.

With this mandate, the team of Sean Cain, E. Don Brown, Mike Laird, and others engaged in an accelerated project to identify the critical practices that separated the consistently successful school and teacher from their less consistent and less successful peers. Early on, the team decided that "success" was not to be defined as the highest raw score on state accountability tests. Such a definition was too heavily aligned to the wealth of a student's family and/or segregative campus programming and design.[1] Instead, the team defined success as a campus or teacher that outperforms a campus or teacher serving similar students. This changed the entire dynamic of the problem. Even now, too many laypeople, politicians, and educators use raw test scores as the primary school and teacher performance indicator. Using this metric, the more affluent almost always outperform the less affluent, be it district, campus, or classroom. Just as segregative campuses, programs, and classrooms almost always outperform open access campuses, programs, and classrooms that serve a more representative sample of the student population.

---

[1] Segregative: A campus, program, or classroom that limits admission to students who meet specific entrance requirements and either does not allow or discourages students who do not meet and/or maintain performance requirements from participating.

When the Innovative School Redesign team began to disaggregate school performance data into similar groups (examples: Title I campus to Title I campus, traditional suburban high school to traditional suburban high school, rural middle school to rural middle school, etc.), a different pattern began to emerge. When similar group data were examined, it became obvious that consistent top performers were less common. When affluent campuses were grouped together, their performance was more alike than not. Pick any disaggregated data group and the patterns were similar, with a few noticeable exceptions. Within a disaggregated group there would sometimes be a school that would remain near or at the top of the disaggregated pack for multiple years. There would also be some schools that consistently underperformed their group. Not year to year random fluctuations, but multiple years being at the bottom or the top of the pack.

It was these observations that drove the initial work of the Innovative School Redesign team. What did the consistently top performing campuses do at greater frequency than the middle of the pack and bottom of the pack performers? What was commonly occurring at the consistently underperforming campus that occurred much less frequently at other campuses? After site visits in scores of school districts and at hundreds of campuses, patterns began to emerge.

Note, these observations occurred in the early 2000s. What is now considered common knowledge was essentially invisible at the time. A few things were obvious almost immediately. First, at every school (except the rare few that had devolved into utter chaos) staff were working hard and trying to educate students. In fact, the more that staff were aware that their jobs were immediately on the line, the harder they were working. In this case, hard work was not a synonym for effective or efficient work but a description of effort. Lack of adult effort was not the driving force behind struggling schools.

Second, the more a school struggled (compared to its similar peers), the less evidence there was of organized, process-driven actions. Third, student demographics masked system failures more than the team ever imagined. This means that a school with fewer instructional delivery and support systems than its peers would consistently underperform its peers.

LEADERSHIP
CONTENT
TEXTBOOKS
PACING
INSTRUCTIONAL PRACTICES
ASSESSMENT
CLASSROOM OBSERVATION

Figure 1.5

However, this underperformance was only highlighted and targeted by the state if *minimum state standards were not being met*. If the student body of a given campus was able to meet minimum state standards, everything was deemed okay. Even if the students on that campus were underperforming their demographic peers attending a similar campus. Translation: An affluent school underperforming its peers faced no state scrutiny or accountability if its students were meeting minimum state performance standards.

As recent former principals—practitioners—as opposed to politicians, researchers, or academics, the team's perspective and understanding of schools was distinct. As soon as the team realized that *relative* low performance and *relative* high performance were not accountability issues but instead universal issues affecting all schools, the team was driven to find the root causes of each. The team made the conscious decision to exceed its mandate.

The team began with a list of observable campus attributes to track. The list was extensive at first but was quickly narrowed down to the following: Leadership, Content, Textbooks, Content Pacing, Instructional Practices, Content Assessment, and Classroom Observations (see Figure 1.5).

Once the list was solidified, observations were collected and sorted, based on where an observed campus was positioned within its disaggregated peer group. Positioning was defined as consistently low performing, consistently performing within the mean, or consistently high performing. Again, it is important to note, this determination was based on a school's performance in relation to its cohorts.[2] A school identified as low performing, *compared to its peers*, was often meeting or exceeding state minimum performance requirements. Figure 1.6 illustrates campus peer groups disaggregated by

	Consistently Low Performing	Consistently Within the Mean	Consistently High Performing
Leadership	Ineffective; Overwhelmed; Revolving Door	Primarily Staff Focused	Primarily Performance Focused
Content	Teacher Determined; Textbook Focused	District or Campus Suggested; Teacher Determined; Textbook Focused	District or Campus Provided Scope and Sequence
Textbooks	Older; Out of Date Adoption; Inadequate Numbers	Up to Date Adoption	Up to Date Adoption
Pacing	Teacher Determined	Teacher Determined	District or Campus Suggested; Teacher Attempt to Implement District Suggestion
Instructional Practices	Teacher Determined	Teacher Determined	Teacher Determined; District or Campus Suggested
Content Assessment	Limited, System-wide Administration of Practice Skills Tests	Semi-Regular, System-wide Administration of Practice Accountability Tests	Mid to Short Term, System-wide Administration of Aligned Content Assessments
Classroom Observation	Limited Number of Summative Observations; All Observations Conducted by Administration	Limited to Required Number of Summative Observations; All Observations Conducted by Administration	Required Summative Observations; Semi-Regular to Regular Formative Observations Conducted by Support Professionals and Administration

Figure 1.6

performance and the observable attributes common within the disaggregated groups.

As the team charted its observations and the data sample grew, certain attributes began to cluster within specific groups. The

---

[2] In sports, if one were to compare *all* football teams, National Football League (NFL) teams are considered the most accomplished. The worst NFL team would beat (outperform) any college team it competed against. Within the peer group of NFL teams, from 2011 to 2020, the Cleveland Browns consistently underperformed.

pattern was not absolute, and every school performing above the mean was doing something typical, or worse. For example, an observed school that was in the "Consistently High Performing" group could have had teacher determined content pacing and no formative classroom observation process. Additionally, schools that were consistently low performing were almost always doing many things that were noticeably ineffective. Again, there were no absolutes, but there were consistent campus process and practice indicators for both high and low performing campuses. The more positive indicators present, the greater the chance that the campus would outperform its peers. The more negative indicators present, the greater the chance that the campus was underperforming its peers. Within a year, the critical, positive attributes aligned with increased school performance were identified, prioritized, and communicated with educators in forums across the state. Now known as **The Foundation Trinity**, these critical system practices are common practice at many schools (see Figure 1.7). At this point, the reader may be wondering, "What does this have to do with **The Fundamental 5?**"

In addition to the above, the team noticed another pattern

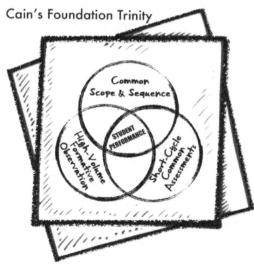

during the process of working to identify what successful schools were doing differently. The team visited multiple campuses every week; campuses that differed in size, grades served, settings, and performance. On those campuses the team informally observed classrooms—well over 100 random teachers a

Figure 1.7 week. With this significant

volume of classroom observations, the team realized that on any given week they observed a handful of truly exceptional teachers. The operational definition of "handful" being five or fewer out of over 100 teachers on multiple campuses. These truly exceptional teachers could pop up anywhere. Campus performance and setting did not seem to be a leading indicator. With this new realization, the team decided to begin to observe teachers using a rudimentary, objective, three-to-five minute, formative observation protocol.

As the overall volume of collected observation data began to increase, a sub-pattern of instructional practice began to emerge in the classes of exceptional teachers. The comparison data (exceptional teacher to typical teacher) indicated two things. One, the exceptional teacher was not doing extraordinary things. Instead, the exceptional teacher was doing ordinary things extraordinarily well. Two, the exceptional teacher was not teaching dramatically differently from the typical teacher. Instead, they were teaching slightly differently at various times during the lesson.

These two observations were paradigm-shifting. Up until that moment, conventional wisdom was that when it came to exceptional teaching, you either had *IT* or you did not. Exceptional teaching was viewed as a magical thing beyond the grasp of mere mortals. Yes, there were still intangibles, but the blueprint for exceptional teaching was right in front of the team and seemingly accessible to everyone. So what was the pattern? What were the ordinary things done extraordinarily well?

First, the exceptional teachers consistently framed their lessons *for the purpose of lesson closure*, over 90% of the time. With the typical teacher, this practice was observed less than 5% of the time. Next, the exceptional teacher was a recognition and reinforcement machine. They engaged in this practice two to four times more often than the typical teacher. They also spent significantly more time in close proximity to students while teaching or monitoring—working in the power zone. The exceptional teacher was observed doing this often at two to three times greater frequency than the typical teacher. The exceptional teacher provided more opportunities for student academic discussions than the typical teacher. Again, often at two to three times greater frequency than the typical teacher. Finally, regardless of content or grade level, the exceptional teacher had students engaged in critical writing activities. Often at three to five times greater frequency than the typical teacher. That is the pattern. That is **The Fundamental 5: Frame the Lesson; Recognize and Reinforce; Frequent, Small Group, Purposeful Talk About the Learning; Critical Writing; and Work in the Power Zone** (Figure 1.8).

Five simple, exceedingly high-yield instructional practices of which the majority of teachers have at least some awareness. Essentially, every teacher uses these practices, occasionally. There is the rub. Extraordinary

Figure 1.8

teachers did not use these five practices occasionally, they used them a lot. Because of this they were much more comfortable with these high-yield instructional practices and therefore used them with greater confidence and quality. This in turn drove improved student responses to the practices. The team was astounded. In their search for the magical, *they stumbled across the do-able.*

Simple Does Not Mean Easy

On paper, **The Fundamental 5** is simple. Five high-yield instructional practices: Frame the Lesson; Recognize and Reinforce; Frequent, Small Group, Purposeful Talk About the Learning; Critical Writing; and Work in the Power Zone. When these five individual high-yield practices are used as a cohesive, integrated unit at high frequency and with high quality, teacher effectiveness is significantly enhanced. Most school administrators want their teachers to adopt most, if not all, of these practices. Most teachers have an awareness of at least some of these practices. Most teachers can reflect on their daily delivery practices and state with complete honesty that they use some of these practices. So simple. Unfortunately, this leads many to believe that better implementation of these practices, individually and collectively, will be easy. This is not the case.

Implementing **The Fundamental 5** at high frequency and with high quality is a function of changing adult behavior. Changing adult behavior is not an easy task, as anyone who has attempted to adopt a diet, an exercise routine, or a New Year's resolution can attest. To change a behavior requires a compelling need, a replacement behavior, and support. The desire to improve pedagogy is a constant. It is the compelling need that is more unique. When a compelling need arose in the past, it was generally localized and in response to coercive pressure. Now the compelling need is universal. Every school, every classroom, and every student has been negatively impacted by the pandemic. Improved pedagogy is the primary COVID-19 gap recovery vehicle available to every teacher. **The Fundamental 5** represent a cohesive package of replacement behaviors that consistently improve the quality of delivered instruction, and, subsequently, student performance. Support is what teachers need in this endeavor. This book is a support; peers are a support; and at enlightened campuses with competent leadership, administration is a support. The more support the teacher has, the greater their chance to significantly improve their craft. Simple, but not necessarily easy.

2 FRAME THE LESSON

If there is a *fundamental one,* it is **Lesson Framing WITH Appropriate Lesson Closure**. Of all the fundamental practices, this is the most incorrect and inconsistent in its implementation. It is also the practice the authors understood the least when they noticed the original pattern of collective, self-reinforcing, best practices—**The Fundamental 5**. Since that time, it is with Lesson Framing that the authors have made the biggest leap in understanding. While they always knew that this was a powerful best practice, they now realize that it is much more powerful than they ever imagined. Statistically, the very few teachers who do this practice, correctly and consistently, reap significant rewards in terms of student performance. Teachers who use the practice inconsistently and/or incorrectly find themselves expending effort, but they are not getting the traction or benefit they expect. Teachers who do not know of the practice or who infrequently attempt it must work harder to make forward progress with their students. This was a poor proposition in the pre-pandemic classroom; post-pandemic it is not sustainable.

What the authors find interesting is that when they talk to educators at conferences and schools, they are constantly being asked, "What's the one thing I can do in my class to improve student performance?"

To which they first reply, "Use **The Fundamental 5** at high frequency and high quality."

This usually gets a polite laugh and the follow up question, "No, really. What's the one thing?"

We understand the question. When trying to improve practice, especially when the teacher is trying to manage the stressful, dynamic, and chaotic environment that is the typical classroom, doing five new things at once is overwhelming. So where should the journey for improved pedagogy begin? That is the critical question— the "one thing" question. Our years of observing, leading, and training teachers has led us to this solid conclusion: the journey for improved pedagogy begins with Lesson Framing with Appropriate Lesson Closure. It is not the only thing, but it is the first thing.

When implemented correctly—*every lesson, every day*—this fundamental practice boosts student engagement, enhances student cognition (rigor), builds and strengthens connections to content (relevance), increases student retention, and facilitates improved content pacing. One practice does all of that, every lesson, every day, for every student. Honestly, if there is any single instructional practice that can be universally implemented and make a bigger impact, we have yet to find it.

Here are some facts to keep in mind as we discuss Lesson Framing with Lesson Closure. First, it is an incredibly effective retention strategy. When teachers Close their lesson appropriately every day, students retain more of what they were taught. When students retain more of what they were taught, the teacher can spend less time reviewing prior content. When teachers do not need to review as often, they are able to teach more new content. As students are taught more new content and retain more of that content, they outperform similar peers who retain less and are taught less.

Second, teachers who consistently and appropriately Frame and Close their lesson have higher observed frequencies of the other four fundamental practices. Tens of thousands of classroom observations conducted since the writing of the first book have led us to realize that teachers who Frame and Close consistently also use the other four practices significantly more often than other teachers. The teacher who Frames and Closes every lesson understands how the other fundamental practices support a strong Close. Because they notice the change in performance, they want even more of the positive change, and this realization drives the following improvements in pedagogy.

As we will discuss in detail later in this chapter, the most common Closure activities are either a quick talking Close with a partner (Frequent, Small Group, Purposeful Talk About the Learning) or a quick written Close (Critical Writing), both of which are **Fundamental 5** practices. Teachers realize that if they want the quality of the talking and writing at the end of the class to be better, then students should have more opportunities to talk and write during the class. As the teacher plans for and provides more opportunities for students to talk and write during the class, the teacher realizes that the quality of the talking and writing improves as they spend more time in the Power Zone. As the teacher spends more time in the Power Zone, observing and supporting students as they engage in Purposeful Talk and Critical Writing, the teacher notices how hard students are working and the incremental growth they are making. As the teacher notices this, they talk to their students, Recognizing their growth and Reinforcing their effort. All of which has the collective effect of increasing the number of students who successfully meet teacher expectations of a quality response to the Close.

Simply put, we now recognize that appropriate and consistent Lesson Framing with Lesson Closure is both the leading indicator and lynch pin of teacher implementation of **The**

Fundamental 5 with increased frequency and quality. Less than 5% of teachers in the field Frame and Close their lesson consistently and correctly. The other 95+% do not. We go as far as to state that this practice of Framing and Closing is the indicator that separates the elite teacher from all the rest. This is a *look in the mirror* moment for all of us in the profession. We can identify the leading indicator that separates the elite teacher (top 5%) from the typical teacher. The leading indicator: Lesson Framing with Appropriate Lesson Closure.

The more a teacher Frames and Closes, the more they use the other **Fundamental 5** practices. The more a teacher uses **The Fundamental 5** practices as an integrated, cohesive unit, the better ALL of their students perform. The better ALL of their students perform, the more the teacher elevates from typical teachers and moves towards the ranks of the elite teacher. If a teacher Frames and Closes their lessons consistently, they are either an elite teacher or moving in that direction. If a teacher does not Frame and Close consistently, they can be hardworking, intelligent, caring, and have the potential to be elite, but they are not elite.

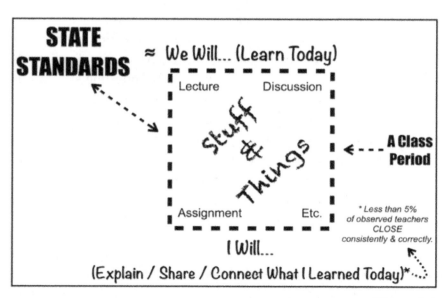

Figure 2.1

A sobering fact is that a large percentage of teachers are aware of Lesson Framing and Closing as an instructional strategy. It has been presented in the literature and trainings as something they could or should do. But it is rarely presented as the *most important* thing they should do. In the rare case it is presented in this way, teachers want to add, "Yes, but...." The "but" is the reason why their content (or students, or performance, or environment) exempts them from the practice. We will be brutally honest with the reader: Lesson Framing with Closure is a critical and fundamental instructional strategy. Its use is appropriate for every subject, grade level, student, and instructional environment. A teacher ignoring this fact pre-pandemic could be politely considered as stuck in their ways. Post-pandemic, this teacher is bordering on professional negligence.

In the past our strongest assets in the classroom were a strong work ethic, a positive connection with students, and a love for our content area. Our instruction was driven by explaining the information from the textbook (lecture and demonstration), assigning individual student work, assisting individual students, trying to keep every student busy working, and assigning what work was not finished as homework. Educational research did not impact daily instruction, and the closest thing to an understanding of Lesson Framing and Lesson Closure in the classroom were the following suggestions:

1. An agenda on the board is useful to some students, and it reminds the teacher of what tasks need to be accomplished during the class period.
2. If there is time, remind students of what they were taught as they leave the class.

Thankfully, awareness and understanding has evolved. Figure 2.1 illustrates this evolution.

Until the 1990s, the center of the learning experience was the class period, represented by the heavy, black dotted line square. In the allotted time of the class period, the teacher was expected to teach an academic subject. To do this, the teacher would develop, design, or borrow activities that they determined would produce the best student outcomes. In less than technical terms, the teacher would fill the class period with Stuff and Things—lectures, discussions, assignments, etc., that promoted learning. As long as the stuff and things the teacher and students were doing were aligned and correlated to the subject, the teacher had made an instructionally sound decision. The algebra teacher did algebra stuff and things in the algebra class, the history teacher did history stuff and things in the history class, and so on. Life was good.

In the mid-to-late 1980s, the education environment began to change. The idea of content standards began to take hold. The short version of the standards movement can be summed up as follows. There is specific content that students need to master as they progress in a subject from grade level to grade level, culminating with graduation. At graduation a random student who passed senior English at School A should have the same base understanding of the English subject as their demographic peer at School B who also passed senior English. If schools can accomplish this, there are significant benefits to society, the economy, and the country. This led to states adopting standards for critical content. First, the four core courses, and now in many states also elective courses. For the record, the adoption of state standards is admirable. However, teaching to these standards is exceedingly difficult in practice. The authors are products of and proponents for content standards. This adoption of state content standards has pushed the profession forward at a rapid pace, and today's students are better educated than yesterday's students and at a far greater and more diverse scale.

With the introduction and adoption of state standards, instructional leaders and teachers quickly realized that the stuff and things that occurred daily in the classroom should directly align with the grade level content standards. It was at this time that campus administrators began pushing teachers to post the state standard on the chalkboard. This was done primarily for administrative purposes. The standards were new and grade level specific. This meant that in almost any classroom an administrator walked into, they would not know if the observed class activity was aligned to the state standard if the standard was not posted for them to see. This is NOT an indictment of campus administrators from that era. Even today's campus administrator does not know every grade level standard for every content. An elementary campus administrator who taught high school biology is not expected to know all third-grade reading standards by heart.

Additionally, if the teacher wrote the state standard on the board, the campus administrator had some assurance that the teacher had at least looked at the state standard and tried to select stuff and things that addressed that standard. This may seem like micromanaging, but, again, the standards were new to both administrators and teachers. Successful implementation did require the purposeful winnowing of irrelevant stuff and things that were content related but not standards focused or aligned.

The progression to this point was: class period with teacher determined stuff and things; to state standards; to a class period with state standard aligned stuff and things and the state standard written on the chalkboard. State standards are written in dry, technical terms for use by educators. They are not written for students. As such, even though writing the state standard on the chalkboard was somewhat useful to a visiting administrator observing a classroom, they were, and still are, of little use to a student. It did not take long for some educators to reach the following conclusion. State standards are useful for planning; state standards written on the board are useful to administrators; state standards written on the board are not useful to students. However, the *translation* of the state standard into *student-*

friendly language (if focused on the day's activities) written on the board is useful to students.

With this almost organic realization, what began to appear on the chalkboard in a lot of classrooms changed. Instead of the formal, technical language of the state standard, exceptional teachers began to translate the standard into student-friendly language. Posted on the board were statements that answered the near universal question, "What are we going to learn today?" To this day, a good objective is the translation of the standard into student-friendly language, specific to today. The younger the student, the more translation is required. The older the student, the less translation is required. Teaching is both a science and an art. With a good objective, the science is the standard. The art is the translation.

This was the education environment that the authors were working in when they began to study classrooms intently. Standards were already in place, the directive to write the state standards on the board was a common practice, and many schools and classrooms had moved or were moving to replace the technical, broad, and formal state standard with a posted, student-centric objective.

In the course of their work, one of the patterns that emerged was related to the objective. Either the state standard or an objective was written on the board in the vast majority of observed classrooms. But in a small percentage of classrooms (1% to 4%), there was something else written. There was a statement or question on the board that the students had to respond to at the end of the lesson every day. This response tied everything that occurred during the lesson together and created a "Hey, I know this" moment for the student. And these classrooms were concentrated in the exceptional performance group. These teachers had figured out the power of consistent, appropriate Lesson Closure. Or, as one teacher explained, "I want my students to think deeply at least once during the class

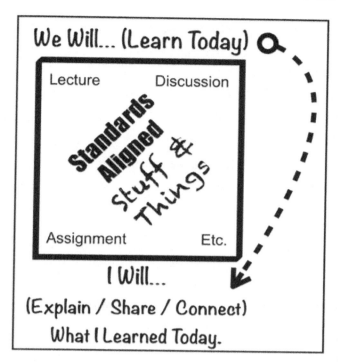

We Will... (Learn Today)

Lecture   Discussion

Standards Aligned *Stuff & Things*

Assignment   Etc.

I Will...
(Explain / Share / Connect)
What I Learned Today.

Figure 2.2

period. So I write on the board what I want them to think about, and then at the end of the class, that is what we do."

Which brings us to the concept of a Lesson Frame. In exceedingly successful classrooms, there were often two statements written on the board. An objective that was correlated to a state standard but written for students. The objective set the stage and answered the "What are we going to do today?" question. There was also a closing question or statement that students responded to at the end of the lesson. These two written statements, **Objective** and **Close**, framed the lesson activities that would occur during the lesson. Hence, the term Lesson Frame was coined. See Figure 2.2. However, one bit of confusion that emerged since **The Fundamental 5** was first published needs to be addressed. The *passive* act of writing a decent Lesson Frame on the board is not the powerful practice. It is the *active and consistent implementation* of the Lesson Frame with Lesson Closure that is the powerful, fundamental practice.

Lesson Framing: A Two Part Best Practice – The Objective

Lesson Framing is a best practice in two parts. The first part of a Lesson Frame is the Objective. The second part is the Close. As we get started, there are five things to keep in mind.

1. This practice, like all **The Fundamental 5** practices, is an active practice and not a passive one. If the use of the practice is passive, it is being implemented incorrectly, and hence ineffectively.
2. Do not overthink the practice. The more complicated a person tries to make the practice, the more ineffective the practice becomes.
3. Follow the script. The more a person improvises, the more ineffective the practice becomes.
4. Be consistent. Correctly implement the practice of Lesson Framing every lesson, every day. Inconsistent implementation ensures that the practice is ineffective.
5. The Lesson Frame is for *students*, not adults.

As stated above, the first part of the Lesson Frame is the Objective. The Objective is a posted and verbalized statement of what students will learn today. It is the *today* part that is most critical. This is not a statement of what students will learn by the end of the unit, this week, or this six weeks. The focus is TODAY's lesson. This is because students live in the present. They do not and cannot know the overall plan for navigating through the course content. It is the adult that must think in terms of multi-day, big picture units of instruction. Then the adult develops daily objectives that support the eventual achievement of longer-term objectives. It is important to remember, on any given day, those longer-term objectives are of little interest and no use to the student. Students simply want and need to know what they will learn today and how they will show it.

Because the Objective is for students, it should be written in student-friendly, concrete, and personal language. Most Objectives are written as a "We will..." statement because its purpose is to communicate to students what we—as a class, a team, a learning tribe—are going to learn today. For example, a teacher could write, "We will learn about the practice of Lesson Framing."

This Objective is direct and to the point. We (the readers of this chapter) are going to learn about Lesson Framing today. Any other information that could be shared at this time about Lesson Framing or any other instructional practice is unnecessary and has the real potential of overwhelming or distracting the student.

There are some common mistakes that teachers make when creating and posting Objectives. The first mistake is that the teacher will not have the Objective posted. Students need to see the Objective when they walk into the classroom and be able to refer to it throughout the lesson. The posted Objective helps to remind students of what they are supposed to learn and re-focus them if their thoughts wander. The Objective should be written BIG and positioned prominently so it can be read from any location in the classroom. The Objective is THE reason for being in class today.

The Objective is generally not written as a high rigor statement. It is usually written at the remembering and understanding level. After all, at the beginning of the lesson, the teacher is working with novices. The rigor will occur in the middle and end of the lesson. The Objective is the set-up. As such, the use of adult-centric or grandiose terms is counter-productive and discouraged. The Objective is for students!

The second mistake teachers make when writing an Objective is using technical language and/or jargon that is unfamiliar to the student. Again, the reader is reminded that the Objective is for the novices in the room and not the experts. Students often have no, little, or incomplete information on what is being taught today (if this is not the case, then why is the information being taught?). The Objective's main purpose is to inform students of what they will learn, today, and get them moving in the right direction. The lesson will then fill in the pertinent information, knowledge, and skills as the class works towards the Close. The Objective is for students!

The third mistake teachers make when writing an Objective is to make it too long and wordy. The authors regularly observe classrooms where the learning objective is paragraph length. Keep in mind, when a student asks a teacher, "What are we going to learn today?" that is the only information they want and need. If the teacher answers the question with a five paragraph answer, the student glazes over and tunes out the teacher. Short and to the point is the rule. The Objective is for students!

The fourth mistake teachers make when writing an Objective is that it is too far reaching. This is the Objective that is used repeatedly for multiple days, an entire week, or an entire unit of knowledge. For example, if the authors were teaching a class on pedagogy, we could write the following Objective on the board, "We will discuss **The Fundamental 5.**" There is nothing inherently wrong with this Objective. If today's lesson is simply a one shot introduction to a body of five practices that when used as a cohesive unit have a significant positive impact on teacher effectiveness and student performance, then the Objective alerts students that some **Fundamental 5** thing will be important today.

However, if **The Fundamental 5** is a topic that will be discussed and explored for multiple lessons, then the Objective, "We will discuss **The Fundamental 5,**" is too far reaching. After the introduction on day 1, the teacher should consider the primary instructional focus of day 2. It could be, "We will examine **The Fundamental 5** practice of Lesson Framing." Now the student is alerted that Lesson Framing is the important concept today. For a later **Fundamental 5** themed lesson, the Objective could be, "We will consider the connection between Lesson Closure and accelerated instruction."

This is where another version of this mistake occurs. The teacher understands that they will cover a lot of important **Fundamental 5** content and concepts for the next couple of days. So on the first day of the unit, they write on the board, "We will discuss **The Fundamental 5**, examine **The Fundamental 5** practice of Lesson Framing, and consider the connection between Lesson Closure and accelerated instruction." Again, this is a mistake.

Yes, knowing that the overall, multi-day instructional unit is a deep dive into **The Fundamental 5**, how it works, why it works, and its impact on content delivery and mastery is important information...but initially only for the teacher, the content expert. For the student, the content novice, the important information for today's class is what will be learned, today. That is the information that is conveyed in a good Objective. Adding more information does not make the Objective more effective, instead it does the opposite. The Objective is for students!

Finally, the last common mistake teachers make when writing an Objective is to make it too generic or writing it in a manner that it could be applied to almost any randomly selected day in the class. For example, a math teacher may write "We will use an array of mathematical strategies to solve a variety of mathematical problems." This is a mistake. Students using math strategies to solve math problems in their math class is a daily occurrence. This Objective uses words but communicates nothing. What would be useful information would be to know which strategy and what type of problem. For example, "We will learn how to use slope to graph a linear equation." The Objective is for students!

Providing students with a crystal clear idea of what they are supposed to learn today impacts students in several positive ways. Knowing that you are about to learn something and what that something will be *primes the brain to be receptive to learning.* The human brain is naturally curious. When someone is made overtly aware that they are about to learn something, they cannot help themselves but to lean in, pay a little more attention, and engage just a little more.

When a teacher simply starts teaching, with little or no introduction of what will be learned today, many students spend a considerable amount of class time confused about what the teacher is talking about, what is going on, and how it connects to anything. When the teacher informs students at the beginning of class what they will learn today, this initial confusion is immediately mitigated. By posting the Objective and verbally communicating the Objective, the teacher is providing a little pre-lesson dose of motivation for the typically unmotivated. The teacher is also providing a little pre-lesson dose of clarification for the typically confused. Now the playing field has been leveled for all students, more students are leaning into the lesson, the entire class begins moving in a forward direction, and the pace of instruction begins to speed up slightly.

The good news is that when teachers are properly trained on how to write an effective, student-friendly Objective, they can do so almost immediately. Writing, posting, and communicating the Objective is the easier part of the Lesson Frame. It also aligns with an existing teacher habit: *Get something on the board so my administrators know that I know what I'm doing today.* The Frame hones that habit into something that is more useful to students and sets up the most important part of the lesson—the Close.

Lesson Framing: A Two Part Best Practice – The Close

To ensure that there is no misunderstanding, the end of the lesson is the most important part of the lesson. If the teacher does every part of the lesson correctly *except* Close, the overall effectiveness of the lesson is diminished. Also, the more at-risk the student, the greater this diminishing effect. If the teacher begins the instructional portion of the class effectively by sharing the Lesson Frame (Objective and Close), stumbles a bit during the meat of the lesson, but Closes the lesson appropriately, the lesson delivery errors are effectively mitigated. Three examples that illustrate the effect of the Objective and Close can be seen in a football game. The Objective of the offense is to move the ball towards the goal line. The Close is to score. The first example is the equivalent of a great lesson with no Close. The ball is snapped. Everything works according to plan. The running back hits the open hole, slips past the linebacker, breaks free in the open field, and runs 50 yards...only to fumble on the one yard line. This is a great lesson with no Lesson Closure.

The second example is the equivalent of a good lesson with a great Close. The offense has the ball, first and goal on the 8-yard line. They run their first play. It works fairly well, gaining four yards. They run their second play, gaining an additional three yards. Now, on third and goal, the running back leaps over the defensive line and scores a touchdown. This is a good lesson with a great Close.

The third example is the equivalent of a less than perfect lesson with a Close. The offense has the ball, first and goal on the 8-yard line. They run their first play. The result is a two yard gain. They run their second play. The result is a one yard loss. They run their third play. The result is another two yard gain. Now facing fourth and goal on the 5-yard line, the team kicks a field goal, putting three points on the score board. This is not the optimal goal of scoring a touchdown, but three points is better than zero points. This is a difficult lesson with an appropriate and effective Close.

The Close, like the Objective, is posted prominently and verbalized. Students must be able to see it throughout the lesson as it is the most important part of the Lesson Frame. It tells the students what they will be required to do at the end of class to demonstrate to their teacher and to themselves that they have learned the most critical aspect of today's lesson and have in fact achieved the Objective. The student knows that they will have to demonstrate, write about, or verbalize the critical understanding or connections from today's lesson. It is the Close that makes this critical knowledge tangible and real in the student's mind and allows them to better connect this to future lessons, knowledge extensions, and experiences.

It is critical that the teacher does everything in their power to ensure that every student engages in the Close because it is during the Close where retention of the content is optimized and maximized. This statement is not made lightly; it is based on an understanding of the primacy/recency effect.[3] The two most vibrant memories of a learning event are what occur first and what occur last. The memory of what occurs in the middle of the learning event gets fuzzy over time. When the teacher presents the Lesson Frame at the beginning of class, it primes the brain for what is to follow, peaks a little interest and curiosity, and makes a *vibrant memory*. This is followed by the lesson and lesson activities, the memory of which is not quite as vibrant and therefore degrades at a more rapid rate over time. If the teacher does not Close the Lesson, there is no distinct end to the activity, just a fading out. Even if a vibrant memory is made, there is no focus to it. If, on the other hand, the teacher appropriately Closes the lesson, the student creates another *vibrant memory* of the critical understandings and/or connections that were the purpose of the lesson and the lesson activities.

When implemented appropriately, the Lesson Frame (Objective and Close) creates the bookends of vibrant memories of content that stay with the student the longest. When students return to class the next day, with stronger connections to and deeper

---

[3] Primacy/recency effect: Information presented at the beginning and end of a learning episode are retained better than the information presented in the middle of a learning episode. Herman Ebbinghaus was the first to write about this, publishing the book *Memory: A Contribution to Experimental Psychology* (1895).

understandings of previous learning, the teacher can leverage those vibrant memories to teach more new content. Most teachers do not Frame or Close correctly, which means that their students never create vibrant memories of deep understandings or connections that are purposefully focused on what is critical in the lesson. Students without these focused vibrant memories are less prepared to resume and continue their learning because they do not clearly remember what they were taught previously. This slows down the pace of learning for the student and the class. Every teacher who experiences the frustration of teaching something to assumed mastery the day before, only to have students seemingly remember nothing today, is suffering the effect of an ineffective or non-existent lesson frame and flawed or non-existent lesson closure. This experience is now labeled the "Exposure With No Closure" effect.

When constructing the Close, the teacher follows guidelines similar to writing an Objective. The Close should be written in concise, concrete, and student-friendly language. The Close is generally written as an "I will…" statement. This statement communicates to the individual student how they will demonstrate the understanding and/or connections they made while completing the lesson activities. For example, in a math class that is just learning how to graph equations, the Objective for a lesson could be, "We will learn how to use slope to graph a linear equation." The Close for this lesson could be, "I will explain to my partner what slope represents and why it is important" or "I will write down how to determine the slope of a line drawn on the coordinate graph."

The lesson activities could include a segment of teacher lecture and demonstration addressing slope and linear equations. There could be a segment of guided practice on graphing lines with a given slope. There could be a segment of partner or individual practice on determining and using slope to draw the graph of a given equation. The teacher would introduce the Lesson Frame (Objective and Close), then the class would engage in the lesson activities. With

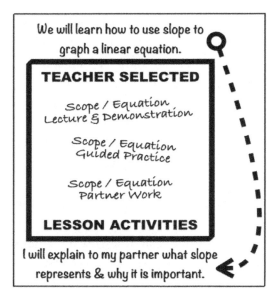

We will learn how to use slope to graph a linear equation.

TEACHER SELECTED

Scope / Equation
Lecture & Demonstration

Scope / Equation
Guided Practice

Scope / Equation
Partner Work

LESSON ACTIVITIES

I will explain to my partner what slope represents & why it is important.

Figure 2.3

three-to-five minutes remaining in the class, the teacher has the students engage in the Close. The Close can only be completed after the lesson activities have occurred because the response to the Close is derived from the understandings and connections the student made while engaged in the lesson activities. See Figure 2.3.

This structure and format works in any class and subject. In a United States history class, the Objective could be, "We will learn about three important events that led to the American Revolution." The selected lesson activities will teach students about those three important events. The Close, which is when students solidify the understanding and connections they made during the exceptional lesson on the lead up to the American Revolution, could be, "I will select the most important event that led to the American Revolution and in three to five sentences justify why I made that selection."

The Close or "I will" statement shared with students at the beginning of the lesson, posted prominently on the board, communicates with each individual student that they are responsible for learning a particular thing today. Additionally, they will demonstrate and articulate that learning by explaining, sharing, and/or connecting what they learned today at the end of today's class. This individual student closing demonstration and articulation of today's learning is generally accomplished through a quick turn-

and-talk with a partner or a quick and targeted Critical Writing activity.

Educators should pay close attention to the following statement to avoid making a common mistake when creating their Close. The Close is *proof of learning or connection*. Students engage in the Close at the end of the class period, after engaging in the various learning activities the teacher selected to teach the Objective. The Close is *not* today's *learning activities*.

Using the above math class example where the lesson Objective is, "We will learn how to use slope to graph a linear equation," the Close is not, "I will take notes on slope and linear equations." The Close is also not, "I will complete the graphing assignment." Both of these are lesson activities. The Close is the demonstration and articulation of the understanding and connections students made while taking notes on slope and completing graphing practice problems. A correct Close would be, "I will explain to my partner what slope represents and why it is important." This represents the critical understanding and connection that the students should walk away with and remember after completing today's lesson activities.

Another commonly observed mistake is the teacher conflating the Close with a task. For example, the teacher may write on the board, "I will complete an exit ticket" or "I will write in my reflections journal." These are tasks. A Close using an exit ticket or a journal might sound like this: "I will summarize slope and its importance in twenty-five or fewer words on an exit ticket (or in my journal)." Students need to be informed of the closing prompt at the beginning of the lesson. This provides the student with a focus and purpose for engaging in the lesson activities. Finally, teachers are reminded that the Close is not the last practice problem. Again, the Close is the demonstration and articulation of the understandings and connections the student gleaned from completing the practice problems.

From a practical standpoint, the end of the lesson is when the student has the most information about the content just taught. This is the point where they can think the deepest about the content and make the strongest connections. This moment is squandered in most classrooms, most of the time. With a purposefully designed and executed Close, the student is positioned to think and connect when they are best able to do so—every lesson, every day. This deep thinking and connection making is also occurring at the same time the brain is naturally making a vibrant memory. Now, not only is recall easier for the student, but the recall is also of deeper understandings of an interconnected web of content, facts, and experiences.

In addition to the student benefits just mentioned, consider the teacher that Closes the lesson consistently and appropriately. This teacher is in the Power Zone (Chapter 6), monitoring responses in real time as students are engaged in the Close. With a talking Close, the teacher listens in on different conversations, strategically targeting the conversations of specific students—the student who typically struggles, the student who is representative of the overall class, and the student who typically excels. With a written Close, the teacher is quickly scanning what students are writing as they are doing it and strategically reading the responses of representative students.

This teacher can use these strategically selected student responses to the Close as real time and accurate formative information. This teacher now knows if most of the students got it. If so, tomorrow the teacher can teach forward, at full speed, and with full confidence. Or the teacher knows which parts of the lesson caused most students to struggle. If so, tomorrow the teacher will reteach these portions of the lesson again, most likely in a slightly different manner. The teacher also knows which students need additional time or support to master the content and makes timely adjustments to delivery, resources, and assignments to better meet these students' instructional needs.

Now consider two similar classes taught by two similar teachers, using similar methods...except Lesson Framing with Appropriate Lesson Closure. Class A and Teacher A will represent a typical classroom and teacher. Class B and Teacher B will represent the classroom and teacher described in the above paragraphs. Teacher A works hard and teaches the required content. The students in Class A diligently listen to their teacher and then work on their daily assignment until the class is over. They quickly gather their materials and move on to the next class. On any given day, a number of students in Class A begin the class slightly confused about what they are doing and why they are doing it. But these students figure it out, eventually. Also, as the year progresses, Teacher A has to spend more time reviewing prior content that students cannot recall at a level adequate enough to support the understanding of new content. This means that either Teacher A has to slow down the pace of new content delivery or keep moving forward to the detriment of an increasing number of students.

Teacher B works hard and teaches the required content. Teacher B begins every lesson by presenting the Lesson Frame. The students in Class B diligently listen to their teacher and then work on their daily assignment until there is five minutes left in the class. At this time Teacher B instructs the class to set aside what they are working on and now address the Close. As students engage in the Close—thinking deeply about what they were just taught, building strong and robust connections to the information, and making vibrant memories of it all—Teacher B is in the Power Zone, monitoring student responses.

On any given day, very few students in Class B begin the class confused, and for those confused students the Lesson Frame generally alleviates this. The instruction provided by Teacher B slowly evolves to better meet the needs of more students. The evolution is driven by ongoing micro-adjustments that are the result of the steady flow of formative information provided to Teacher B by the Close. Also, as the year progresses, Teacher B begins to teach more new content as the students are able to assimilate information at an improved pace due to both their improved retention of prior content and their deeper understanding of it. By the end of the year, in Class B more students have learned more content at higher levels of mastery than in Class A. Two similar classes taught by two similar teachers; by the end of the school year, two dramatically dissimilar results.

Lesson Framing: Language Matters

A Lesson Frame is not for the teacher and not for any other educator that might visit the classroom. These adults already have an advanced understanding of the content. A Lesson Frame is for students! Because the Lesson Frame is for students, the language used matters. See Figure 2.4.

Figure 2.4 shows an actual mathematical standard. *The student shall apply mathematical process standards to develop foundational concepts of functions.* This standard, depending on the students being taught, might be the focus of the class for two or three weeks or longer. The language is impersonal, addressing the generic "student." The language is abstract, addressing broad "process standards." The language is clinical, stating "the student shall apply," similar to the instructions one would find on a tube of ointment. The language is technical. It is neither flawed nor incorrect, but this standard was written by content experts for an audience of content experts to read and use...*not students*. This impersonal, broad, abstract, clinical, and technical standard is of no interest and relevance to essentially any student, *and* it can be intimidating for younger and/or less accomplished students. This is why the authors recommend that teachers do *NOT* write the state standard on the board.

Figure 2.4 also shows a Lesson Frame that addresses the component of the state standard that will be taught today. Written in concrete and personal language, it represents the translation of the standard into student-friendly language that provides relevant information. The Objective: *We will learn how slope helps us graph an equation.* The Close: *I will explain to my partner what slope represents and why it is important.*

LANGUAGE MATTERS	
STATE STANDARD:	**LESSON FRAME:**
The student shall apply mathematical process standards to develop foundational concepts of functions.	**We will learn how slope helps us graph an equation.**
	I will explain to my partner what slope represents and why it is important.
◆ Impersonal	☑ Personal
◆ Abstract	☑ Concrete
◆ Clinical	☑ Real Life, Real Time
◆ Technical	☑ Conversational
◆ **Less Useful to Students**	☑ **More Useful to Students**

Figure 2.4

After reading and hearing this Lesson Frame, every student knows what they will be learning and working on today (slope) and what they will have to do at the end of the lesson (explain slope and its importance to a partner). Now consider the language of the Lesson Frame. "We" and "I" are first person language that speaks directly to the students. "We" communicates to the students what they are going to learn today with the active involvement of the teacher. "I" communicates to the students that they, personally, are responsible for demonstrating learning in some form at the end of today's lesson.

This language is concrete, the students are learning something specific (slope), and something specific will be done with this new knowledge (explain it and its importance to a partner). This language is real and relevant. The students are learning something and doing something with it, today. This language is conversational, not overly technical, and not "dumbed down." Mathematical vocabulary, such as slope, graph, and equation, are used but communicated in a less intimidating and more positive manner. To write this Lesson Frame, the teacher must know the state standard in full depth and detail. That is the job of the teacher (i.e., the content expert). The student needs to know today's learning journey and destination. With that useful information and minimal distraction, students have a better chance to successfully navigate through new information and create deeper understandings.

Lesson Framing: Consistent Implementation

Now that the reader has a better understanding of Lesson Framing, a quick summary is in order. A Lesson Frame is a best instructional practice, consisting of two parts, an Objective and a Close. It is an active practice. It is not enough to write a Lesson Frame on the board. A Lesson Frame is posted and communicated, and students are aware of it and able to use the information it provides. Most importantly, the teacher implements the Close and students engage in the Close every lesson, every day. The Objective is derived from the standard, written in concrete student-friendly language, and it is specific to today. The Close, also written in concrete student-friendly language, provides the means for students to demonstrate or articulate the critical understandings and connections they made from engaging in today's lesson activities.

Writing a decent Objective is not a difficult task if the teacher follows these recommendations.[4]

---

[4] A decent Objective is all that is required. If the Objective is understood by the student and is specific to today, it meets the necessary requirements. The extra time

THE FUNDAMENTAL 5 REVISITED

1. Review the standards correlated lesson plan. This assumes there is a standards correlated lesson plan. If there is not, then build one.

2. Imagine that a student asks the universal question, "What are we going to learn today?"

3. Think of the answer to that question, based on the review of the lesson plan.

4. Write the answer to the question down in the form of a "We will…" statement.

5. Confirm that the "We will…" statement is written in student-friendly, concrete language that is accessible to the students and is specific to the day the lesson will be delivered.

6. Congratulate yourself! You have just written a decent Objective.

This decent, daily Objective is important. When prominently posted and presented to students at the beginning of class, it reduces the level of confusion for some students, provides a small dose of motivation to other students, and relieves some of the stress that confused and under motivated students often experience. Essentially, the teacher has leveled the playing field for students in the classroom. Additionally, the Objective serves as a touchstone throughout the lesson. As points are made in class, the teacher can tie them back to the Objective with a "Yes, that is right in line with the Objective and will be helpful when we get to the Close."

While the Objective is important, the most critical component of the Lesson Frame is the Close. The Close occurs in the last two to five minutes of the daily content delivery period. It is during the Close that all students articulate and/or demonstrate the key understandings and connections from the lesson. It is during the

---

required to create a "great" Objective is better used on lesson design and/or the Close.

Close where a vibrant memory of today's content, understandings, and connections is created. It is the Close that provides the teacher with critical formative information. The teacher is in complete control of whether or not the Close occurs in every lesson, every day.

There are two primary vehicles for the learner to articulate their understanding of the lesson during the Close. The first is the quick partner talk, which generally takes only one to three minutes. Group size for a talking Close should be limited to two students (unless there is an odd number of students, then a single group of three will be necessary). With a talking Close, the instructional goal is to get every single student to engage with the Close and talk. The other primary vehicle for Lesson Closure is the critical quick write/exit ticket. With a

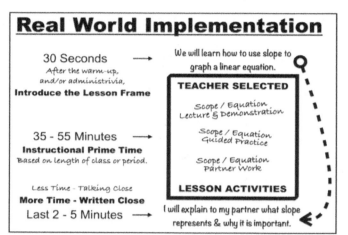

Figure 2.5

written Close, more time is allotted with three to five minutes generally being adequate. With a written Close, the instructional goal is to get every single student to engage with the Close and write.

The most important element of the Close is to actually do it. A great Close on the board that is not implemented is simply camouflaged bad instructional practice. Educators often tell us, "We agree with you. We want to do it. We just do not have the time."

The lack of time defense is seemingly legitimate. In general, class periods have been shortened, course standards have expanded and are more rigorous, and student performance requirements have increased. Translation: Teachers have to successfully teach more content, at higher levels of cognition, to more students, *in less time*. It hardly seems fair. However, because this is the reality for today's teachers, they actually do not have time to *not* Frame and Close their lessons. If teachers are required to cover more content, and students are expected to retain more content the first time they hear it— Frame and Close. If teachers need more students to think deeper about content more often—Frame and Close. If teachers need more students to perform at higher levels when assessed on required content standards—Frame and Close. Lesson Framing and Lesson Closure are the workable solution to the legitimate teacher problems of more work and less time. Figure 2.5 is a visual representation of how to accomplish this.

In most classrooms teachers are allotted 45 to 65 minutes to teach their content.[5] As soon as the teacher completes required administrivia and a warm-up, the teacher should introduce the Lesson Frame.[6] This should take no longer than 30 seconds. Some teachers have a student read the Lesson Frame. This is acceptable if it takes no more than 30 seconds.

The next 35 to 55 minutes of class time (dependent on the overall length of allotted class time) is instructional prime time. This is the time when the teacher and students engage in the instructional stuff and things that the teacher has selected to teach the lesson.

With two to five minutes of class time remaining, the teacher has the students stop whatever instructional stuff and thing they are

---

[5] With a secondary A/B Block schedule, many believe that teachers are allotted 90 minutes to teach a lesson. This is incorrect. In an A/B Block schedule, teachers meet with their students every other day. Teachers should teach two lessons in their allotted 90 minutes. This means that they still only have 45 minutes allotted to teach a lesson (90 minutes/2 lessons = 45 minutes per lesson).

[6] Administrivia: In the classroom, this would be daily activities like taking roll, collecting homework, doing lunch counts, etc.

working on and engage in the Close. A talking Close usually requires just two to three minutes. A written Close generally requires three to five minutes.

For many teachers this stopping part is a difficult thing to do. Once students are engaged and working on academic practice assignments, teachers just cannot seem to stop the students. Instead, the bell stops the class. Teachers must stop the academic practice with enough time to Close correctly. No matter what assignment students are working on or how hard they are working on it, it is *not as powerful* as a correctly implemented Close. Skipping the Close so students can complete one or two more practice problems is a bad trade. It is the equivalent of choosing two pennies instead of one nickel because two seems better than one. One more practice problem does not make much of a difference when the student has already completed nine practice problems. What will make a difference is when the student thinks deeper, ties everything together, and creates a vibrant memory while completing the Close at the end of every lesson, every day.

2 + 2 + 1 = *The Consistent and Powerful Close*

When the authors first observed the early adopters of Lesson Closure, we did not realize that these observed teachers were fully formed. Not only had these teachers progressed through the learning curve, but because most of them had figured out the practice organically, they did not realize that there had even been a learning curve. As such, we simply reported what we observed. Additionally, because we had been observing the practice and its effect on student performance, we took the model of the early adopters and replicated the practice in the classrooms and training rooms where we continued to teach.

When typical teachers begin to implement the practice of Lesson Framing, they go through a predictable, and often slow, learning curve. In the Lesson Framing process, there is a lot of doing it wrong until it is done right. And the doing it wrong part of the process does not produce significant changes in student performance, which means a lot of teachers abandon the Lesson Framing practice. It is our intent to speed up the learning for the reader to avoid the *work but no results* segment of the learning curve and get right to the *work with positive results* learning curve segment.

The following are the typical observed stages of Lesson Framing adoption.

- Stage 1: The teacher writes statements on the board that resemble the Lesson Frame structure. They write something that resembles an Objective. They write something that resembles a Close. Without coaching or support, many teachers will not progress beyond this stage. If a teacher remains at this stage, they are putting forth greater effort than any results they get in return.

- Stage 2: The teacher writes statements on the board that begin to adhere to the Lesson Frame format. What is intended to serve as the Objective is written as a "We will" statement. What is intended to serve as the Close is written as an "I will" statement. Without coaching or support, many teachers will not progress beyond this stage. If a teacher remains at this stage, they are putting forth greater effort than any results they get in return.

- Stage 3: The teacher writes a decent Objective in the correct format on the board. The Close is written in the correct format, but it does not represent proof of understanding or connection. Instead, it communicates the lesson activity. "I will complete the water cycle worksheet" is a representative example of this common mistake. By Stage 3, the teacher is often verbalizing the Lesson Frame for students at the beginning of class. Without coaching or support, many teachers will not progress beyond this stage. If a teacher remains at this stage, they are putting forth greater effort than any results they get in return.

- Stage 4: The teacher writes a decent Lesson Frame on the board. The Close, *if attempted*, would be appropriate. The teacher presents the Lesson Frame to students at the beginning of class. The teacher does *not* Close. Very few teachers progress past this stage. They have done all the work to get to this point, but the performance rewards are in the next stage. Is it any wonder why most teachers abandon the practice? Four stages of hard work and little reward to show for it.

Now for the learning curve acceleration. We previously shared the steps for creating a decent Objective. The teacher who follows those steps is starting their learning curve at Stage 3. Creating an effective, powerful Close for every lesson boils down to the teacher following a simple formula: *2 + 2 + 1*.

For the first "2," the teacher has to make a decision. For the planned Close, the teacher decides if students will talk to a partner (talking Close) or complete a critical quick write (written Close). Both of these options are good. A teacher could have students engage in a talking Close every day, and their students would outperform previous levels experienced by the teacher. A teacher could have students engage in a written Close every day, and their students would outperform many of their peers. This would include their peers who engaged in a daily talking Close. A written Close is more powerful than a talking Close. A talking Close is more effective than *no* Close.

After the teacher decides if they will have a talking or written Close, they must decide what the students will talk or write about. The second "2" requires the teacher to select one of two prompts. The two options are either some form of a summarization prompt or some form of a similarities and/or differences prompt. A summarization prompt is good, better than almost all other Closing prompts. A similarities and/or differences prompt is *even better* than a summarization prompt. All other lesser prompts are better than *no* prompt.

The "1" in the 2 + 2 + 1 formula is not a choice. It is an absolute. If the teacher is to Close their lessons consistently, day in and day out, they must use a *timer*. Any timer, a traditional kitchen timer, an on-line timer, or a smart phone timer. A timekeeper can be an assigned student job. It is critical that the teacher have something to alert them that it is time to Close. What is clearly observable is that the teachers who Close consistently use some form of a timer. Teachers who do not Close consistently do not use a timer.

Why is this the case? The reality is that the modern classroom is too

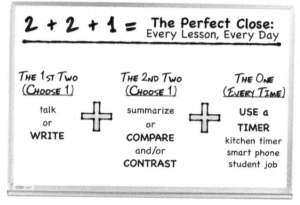

Figure 2.6

stressful, too dynamic, with too many moving parts, and too many demands for the teacher to be able to reliably manage time to the exact minute. If the teacher is experiencing one of those days where everything is working perfectly, time flies by even faster than expected. Without a timer, the typical teacher is surprised by the bell more times than not. The only solution...use a timer. What we know is *no timer = no closure*. No matter what the teacher has written on the board. See Figure 2.6.

Resist the urge to overcomplicate the 2 + 2 + 1 formula. It has been purposefully refined to ensure that the teachers who use the formula get the greatest possible results, every time. Some teachers have asked if following the formula every day becomes boring or stale for students. The answer to this question is "No." Even if the same prompt and format is utilized at the end of every lesson, the specifics of the content change every day, which means that students have to produce a different response every day. There are other teachers who claim to feel constrained by the formula because it "stifles" their creativity. Our response is direct and straightforward: If the creative solution is always less effective than the formulaic solution, then save the creativity for when it matters. In this case, be creative in the development of lesson activities. Close using the 2 + 2 + 1 formula to position students to create vibrant memories of what they just learned from doing the creative activities.

The teacher who follows the 2 + 2 + 1 formula, day in and day out, has separated themselves from the ranks of the typical teacher. The teacher that Closes every lesson with a form of written summarization is positioning students to build vibrant memories of content as they engage in the second most powerful instructional practice. This is the equivalent of hitting a home run, every game, every day. The teacher that Closes every lesson with a form of written similarities and/or differences is positioning students to build a vibrant memory of content as they engage in the most powerful instructional practice. This is the equivalent of hitting a grand slam home run, every game, every day.

Closing with written summarization or written similarities/differences is difficult with young students. For that reason, we provide the following grade level recommendations for written Close frequencies. For early primary grades (pre-kindergarten, kindergarten, and 1st grade), a written Close is a rare occurrence. This is because early writers are not developmentally ready to transfer thoughts and spoken words into writing. As such, Closure in these grades is almost exclusively a talking Close or a demonstration Close (to be discussed later in this chapter). For 2nd grade, it is recommended that a written Close be used once a week in every academic course. For 3rd grade, it is recommended that a written Close be used twice a week in every academic course. For grades 4 through 12, it is recommended that a written Close be used at least 60% of the time (three or more times a week) in every academic course. These recommendations are based on the significant power of Critical Writing balanced against the writing skills of the typical student in each grade level.

For students with special needs or who have exceptional difficulties writing, a talking Close is always appropriate. However, there is a difference between a student with exceptional difficulties writing and a student who finds writing difficult. Often what causes a student to find writing difficult is the lack of writing practice and writing opportunities. The solution to this is more writing practice, more writing opportunities, and more teacher support, all of which are provided in the classroom of a teacher who utilizes a high volume of written Closes. A good rule of thumb is the more at-risk the student, the more the written Close is needed in the class.

Lesson Closure and the Performance Class

In academic classrooms, the primary closure vehicles are the talking and written Close. These are quick and natural practices in information-centric academic settings. This fit is not as natural in a performance class. What is a performance class? It is a class where the demonstration of mastery is often the performance of a discrete and physical skill or task. Examples of performance classes are art, choir, band, vocational courses, physical education courses, kindergarten, etc. In these courses the Close could be, "I will use manipulatives to show 2 groups of 7" (kindergarten), "I will complete a straight weld" (vocational), or "I will dribble the basketball through the cones" (physical education).

With a demonstration Close, the teacher, director, or coach observes the student performance at the end of the class (or practice) and often provides some quick feedback on the quality or improvement of the performance. As the teacher, director, or coach observes the student performances, they make real time decisions on what the focus or practice will be in the next class, based on the students' current skill level. We also recommend the following addition to the performance Close. When students are engaged in a performance Close, they are generally operating at the applying level of cognition. If an analysis level talking prompt is added to the performance Close, the positive effect of the practice can be magnified. An example of this could be as simple as, "I will complete a straight weld and then explain to my partner what my focus was as I did it."

It is common in performance classrooms for students to work on a skill or project for an extended period of time. An example could be a student working on a painting assignment for multiple days in an art class. In this situation, we recommend that teachers use quick talking Closes that position students to analyze their decision making or consider what they would do in a different situation. In the case of the painting assignment example, on Day 1 the art teacher could Close with, "I will explain to my partner why I chose this subject." Later in the project the art teacher could Close with, "I will explain to my partner why I chose this perspective" or "I will explain to my partner how I would present my piece to a master painter for critique." The purpose for Closing in this way is to position students, who by the nature of the activity are operating at the application level of cognition, to stretch their thinking to the analysis level or higher.

Another common activity in performance classes is the group or team performance. This would be the band preparing for a performance, the drama class rehearsing for a play, or the volleyball team practicing for the next game. With a group or team performance, the standard Lesson Frame and Lesson Closure format at times does not quite work. Consider how bands typically practice. Often, groups of students practice on their instruments and work on their piece of the group performance in sectional practice. This does not lend itself to a "We will" statement. At the end of the practice, the band comes together as a group to play a piece of music. This does not lend itself to an "I will" statement. In this commonly observed circumstance, flip the Lesson Frame format. Write the Objective for the lesson (practice) as an "I will" statement. "I will practice the beginning of my part of *The Horse*."[7] That practice is what will occupy the student for most of the class. Write the Close for the lesson (practice) as a "We will" statement. "We will play the first part of *The Horse* paying particular attention to the beat." The band playing together at the end of the practice is the performance Close. The quality of the performance provides immediate feedback to the musicians, and the band director knows exactly what will be worked on during the next practice.

Framing the Lesson in the Remote Classroom

A Lesson Frame is a valuable instructional resource that directs students to the primary learning objective in a virtual/remote lesson. The Lesson Frame creates and maintains the expectation that all students will not only participate in the Lesson Closure but are responsible for quality thinking and/or connections. Student engagement is significantly enhanced throughout the lesson, and this is especially important since the teacher's passion, personality, and proximity are muted in the challenging instructional environment that is the remote classroom.

During the lesson, having the Lesson Frame visible from time to time, either on a whiteboard shown on camera, a repeating message in a chat box, or embedded in the footer of a presentation slide, provides students with a subtle nudge back towards the

---

[7] James, J. (1968). "The Horse" [Recorded by Cliff Nobles and Company]. *Love is All Right* [B-side]. Philadelphia, PA: Phil-L.A. of Soul Records.

teacher's planned learning path. Regardless of the way the Lesson Frame is presented to the students, the critical factor is the students are aware of the Lesson Frame, can at various times throughout the lesson see the Lesson Frame, and understand that they will participate in the Close. In the virtual classroom with Lesson Frame utilization, overt and redundant should be the standard practice. The Lesson Frame is for students!

In a virtual instructional environment, where the students are removed from the teacher, connecting the purpose of the lesson and how the students will demonstrate their learning is critical. The purpose of the Lesson Frame is to help students focus on the content understanding or connections they are expected to possess by the end of the lesson. Even in a virtual/remote learning environment, the Close must occur and all students must participate. To ensure that this occurs, teachers are encouraged to use many of the same techniques and routines that are used to Close consistently in a face-to-face setting. Use and display a timer and use the last presentation slide to remind the teacher and the students when to engage in the Close. These techniques ensure that the Close is not overlooked and that students have a clear understanding of what they are expected to produce and in what format (see Figure 2.7), be it written or verbal. A verbal Close requires the use of a breakout room feature.

Lesson Closure in the remote environment with grade 3 – 12 students tends to lean on the written Close. The primary format for this written Close will be the critical quick write, discussed in detail in Chapter 5. Examples of a quick write Closure include students completing a Venn diagram, a T-chart (both are quick forms of written similarities and differences), or answering a closing prompt in 25 words or less (a quick form of summarization). In a synchronous remote setting, many teachers have access to classroom sharing platforms and chat box features that allow students to type in their written Close response and have it accessible for immediate review. If such a tool is not available, we have observed a number of teachers successfully implement the low tech solution of having students write their response to the Close in big letters on a piece of paper, individual whiteboard, or even a disposable plastic plate. After completing the Close, the teacher has every student hold what they wrote in front of their device camera for the teacher to see.

If a breakout room or similar feature is available, the teacher has the option to use a talking Close. This may add some monitoring difficulties that the following suggestions might mitigate. Type the closing prompt in a message box that students can see while in the breakout room. Before releasing students to their breakout rooms, announce that two or three designated groups will be expected to share the highlights of their discussion. Then, if possible, pop into various breakout rooms to monitor the conversations that are occurring.

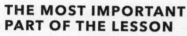

THE MOST IMPORTANT PART OF THE LESSON

In 2 to 4 Sentences in the Chat Box...

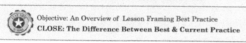

I will highlight the significant differences between the CLOSE as it should be implemented and what has typically occurred at the the end of a lesson in my classroom (or on my campus).

Objective: An Overview of Lesson Framing Best Practice
CLOSE: The Difference Between Best & Current Practice

Figure 2.7

There is a hybrid vehicle for remote environment Lesson Closure that a number of teachers used in asynchronous settings. After observing the lesson and completing the lesson activities, the student would respond to the Close in a quick recorded video. Usually taking less than a minute, the student would verbalize their understanding of the lesson or the connections they made during the lesson. Essentially a Closing monologue, this format allows the student who is working alone to state out loud what they learned. By doing so, the student is able to crystalize a figurative, mental cloud of abstract ideas and concepts into usable, tangible knowledge.

The Lesson Frame (displayed and verbalized) and a completed Close are powerful in the best of instructional settings. In more adverse instructional settings (see: virtual instruction), the use of this **Fundamental 5** practice is the difference between occupying required time and actual teaching and learning.

3 RECOGNITION AND REINFORCEMENT

After writing **The Fundamental 5**, the authors have continued their work in schools across the country, conducting tens of thousands of classroom observations to collect objective formative data. With their continued study of **Recognition and Reinforcement**, as with Lesson Framing, the authors' understanding of the critical elements of the practice has grown and evolved. We now have a better understanding of why this practice works and why close approximations of the practice are not as effective.

When asked to self-report on their use of Recognition and Reinforcement, teachers reported their use at significantly higher levels than our field observations would indicate. What the authors came to realize was that teachers do not Recognize and Reinforce their students in the specific and precise definition of this educational best practice. Instead, they engage in the lesser practice (in terms of improving performance) of positive talk. Engaging in classroom positive talk is good. From a classroom climate standpoint, it is a better practice than neutral talk and a significant upgrade from negative talk. However, positive talk does not produce the improved academic benefit of frequent and effective Recognition and Reinforcement.

Positive Talk

What is positive talk? It is general, non-individualized, and/or non-specific positive statements. For example, a teacher saying, "Hey, everybody, good job" or "I like the way everyone is working" are both examples of positive talk heard in many observed classrooms.

While positive talk sets an overall pleasant tone in the classroom, these are general statements that have little impact on individual students. The student or students the teacher is actually trying to praise are not quite sure if the teacher means them. Also, almost without fail, the student or students the teacher does not want to praise have been lumped into the group and will believe that the teacher means only them. Additionally, what exactly is the good job or the acceptable way of working referenced in the above examples? In the students' minds, it is whatever they happen to be doing at the time they hear the teacher speak. These broad, imprecise statements provide little meaning or feedback, and hence, they do not result in students replicating the desired behavior or academic practice at increased levels. We now recognize and understand that authentic, academic Recognition and Reinforcement is a form of positive talk, but positive talk is not academic Recognition and Reinforcement.

Academic Recognition and Reinforcement

Academic Recognition is the *personal* and *specific* recognition of academic *growth* or academic *success*. Of these two categories, it is the recognition of academic growth that provides the greatest performance boost in the typical classroom. As educators, we generally do an adequate job of recognizing those students who have made it to the top of the academic mountain. We celebrate the students who make an A on the test, make the Honor Roll, or have the highest class rank. Adults and the education system provide these students with regular doses of recognition. Unfortunately, this is often an all or nothing proposition. Frustratingly, a small percentage of the student body receives recognition for what adults consider exceptional academic success, which leaves a majority of the student body with next to no recognition because they rarely, or never, cross the system defined "exceptional" threshold.

As educators, we all too often overlook the students who have made measurable gains while progressing up the mountain. This oversight must be corrected because these are the students who benefit the most from the deliberate use of personal and specific Recognition of academic growth. This practice is a powerful motivator that keeps students engaged in the climb. Yes, the overall academic success of a top student is important. But considerably more important is entire groups of previously underperforming students making significant academic gains. What separates the great teacher from the typical teacher is not the performance of the student who would be successful in any class. It is the successful performance of the students in their class that would not be nearly as successful in any other teacher's class.

Now that academic Recognition has been defined, what exactly is authentic, academic Reinforcement? Authentic, academic Reinforcement is the personal and specific reinforcement of the work and/or effort necessary to achieve a level of academic growth or success. In other words, the teacher is specifically reinforcing a particular student for their persistence, not giving up, sticking to it, continuing to try, and giving sweat equity when they could stop—especially when quitting would be the easiest thing to do. Even when this intense and ongoing effort is not yet producing the improvement and results that the student immediately expects, the teacher that provides authentic, academic Reinforcement to their students helps keep them motivated to stay engaged in the learning process.

To clarify, what separates the high-yield instructional practices of authentic, academic Recognition and Reinforcement from the more typically observed classroom practice of positive talk is the individualization, specificity, and academic focus. "Good job, class" is a positive talk statement directed at everyone, which also means effectively no one. "Good job" also lacks a specific academic activity in which to tie the statement. Is the "good job" for the student using descriptive language in the paragraph they are writing? Or is the "good job" for the student who is supposed to be working on the same assignment but is instead writing "AC/DC Rules" over and over on their paper.[8] The teacher might know, but the students do not.

Authentic, academic Recognition and Reinforcement is directed towards a specific student and addresses specifically what that student is doing that is worthy of the Recognition and/or Reinforcement. An example of this might sound like, "Rian, I like your use of figurative language in this paper. It really helps the reader feel what you are writing about and makes them want to keep reading." It is crystal clear to Rian that the teacher is addressing her, and her use of figurative language is making her writing better.

In this same class, you might hear the teacher say, "Caleb, I know that the assignment was difficult, but you didn't give up. Even when I could tell that you were getting frustrated. That's why your grades are improving." By talking to Caleb in this way, the teacher is helping Caleb see the connection between his effort and his improving grades. Even if he and the teacher are not satisfied with his current performance, he is beginning to realize that it is his hard work that is the critical variable in his overall success.

With this new understanding of the difference between positive talk and Recognition and Reinforcement, let us compare the classroom observation data between a typical teacher and an exceptional teacher. Typical and exceptional describe the differences

---

[8] AC/DC is a heavy metal rock band that was popular in the 1980s. The authors are old.

in frequency of an observed practice.[9] With enough data, a graph similar to Figure 3.1 will emerge.

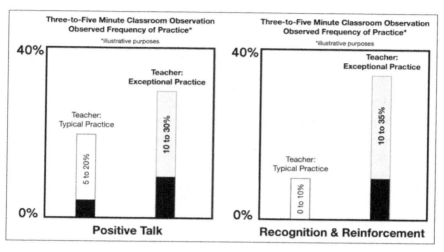

Figure 3.1

Consider the graph comparing positive talk frequency. The typical teacher will be observed using positive talk during 5% to 20% of the observations, with more elementary teachers at the higher end of the range and more secondary teachers at the lower end of the range. With exceptional teachers, the positive talk frequency ranges between 10% and 30%, with a similar elementary/secondary pattern in the data present. This does not mean that the rest of the time teachers are engaged in "negative talk." Teachers are rarely observed

---

[9] The authors use the **PowerWalks Formative Classroom Observation System** to collect data. **PowerWalks** is a very powerful and precise three-to-five minute classroom observation protocol where the observer marks only what occurs during the actual observation. There is no judgement assigned in the observation, and it is understood that no meaningful interpretation of the data can occur until a statistically significant sample of observations have been collected. For an individual teacher, a statistically significant sample would be approximately 20 observations conducted over a six-to-nine week period. The authors have used versions of this observation protocol for over ten years and have collected classroom observation data from tens of thousands of classrooms across the country.

displaying this behavior. Instead, it means that they are engaged in neutral, task oriented, and/or friendly talk.

Now consider the graph comparing the frequency of observed Recognition and Reinforcement. In the typical teacher's classroom, authentic, academic Recognition and Reinforcement is not exactly common, with occurrence rates ranging between 0 and 10%. In the exceptional classroom, the practice is observed 10% to 35% of the time. What is interesting is that the elementary/secondary skewing that is evident in the positive talk frequency is absent. The teachers that Recognize and Reinforce their students do so because at some level they recognize the power of the practice and use it purposefully. This is especially evident in the classrooms where the practice is occurring at the very top of the frequency range. The practice is so common in these classrooms that one assumes that the students would become numb to the practice. In fact, it seems that the opposite occurs. The more the teacher Recognizes and Reinforces their students, the more the students do to receive additional Recognition and Reinforcement.

This observation has led the authors to give the following advice when they are asked what a teacher should do to better prepare students in the last couple of weeks prior to state exams. The question is asked numerous times as state testing season approaches and the authors' response is always, "When it is crunch time, the teacher should Close every lesson and Recognize and Reinforce like a machine. The students will retain more of what was taught and put forth an honest effort." What teacher does not want that?

For those who want to use the above data as a slight against today's classroom teachers, the authors would like to point out that the frequency of observed positive talk and Recognition and Reinforcement for all teachers has increased since we began collecting classroom observation data in the early 2000s.

The body of education research on effective pedagogy consistently ranks academic Recognition and Reinforcement as the third most powerful instructional strategy. The short version of the research clearly prompts teachers with, "Teach what you have always taught. Teach it the way you have always taught it. Recognize and Reinforce your students more, and your students will give you more."

Our more effective teachers have figured this out. They either did this intuitively, read about the practice, or they were trained how to do the practice. But after they figured it out, regardless of how, they used the practice, and they used it a lot, especially when compared to their typical peers. Because they Recognize and Reinforce their students a lot, their students work longer, with greater intensity, and with more persistence than they do in other classrooms. The result of this better effort is student performance that is measurably better than similar students taught the same subject by a different teacher who does not provide a high volume of Recognition and Reinforcement.

As teachers work to implement this **Fundamental 5** practice with increased frequency and quality, they also build and support other elements of a desirable, healthy classroom environment. This is the primary reason Recognition and Reinforcement is a *fundamental* practice. Not only does it provide direct academic benefits, but the practice also contributes in other ways, referred to as soft benefits. First, as a teacher increases both the quantity and quality of Recognition and Reinforcement, this improves the relationships between the teacher and their students. It shifts the typical Teacher/Student relationship to a more dynamic Mentor/Mentee relationship. Students naturally gravitate to those teachers that they connect with and believe will make them more successful. The teacher providing a high volume of Recognition and Reinforcement to students makes students want to connect with that teacher. Students, like all humans, crave Recognition and Reinforcement. The more they get it, the more they do the things necessary to get more of it. Which in turn, by doing those things, makes them more successful. Which then means they get additional Recognition and Reinforcement. Yes, this is a self-replicating pattern.

Recognition and Reinforcement is a powerful teacher tool for building and nurturing motivated students. As students experience the positive feelings that are associated with success and growth and have that experience intensified by the frequent, personal, specific Recognition and Reinforcement provided by the teacher, they begin to connect those positive feelings to the work itself. As this occurs, students begin to willingly engage in the work activity because it allows them to replicate those good feelings. As they engage in the work, they *feel* the powerful words previously spoken by the teacher, which provides an internal motivation for them to remain on task longer and continue to try, even when facing adversity. At this point, students become more willing to take risks in the classroom. They are more willing to put themselves out there because they know the repercussions of failure are minimized and temporary. What matters now is that the students are working hard and are willing to engage in ever increasingly difficult tasks and assignments. Students begin to realize that doing something, even if done poorly, is just the first step on the journey to success. The constant and effective Reinforcement of their efforts, along with constant and effective Recognition of intermediate accomplishment and growth, makes the journey much more important than the destination. This allows any student to progress faster and further than their peers in other classrooms where Recognition and Reinforcement is infrequently used or nonexistent.

Improved student *loyalty* towards their teacher is an additional dynamic that the increased use of Recognition and Reinforcement has on a class. Students become increasingly loyal to the educators that they believe have helped or are helping them improve and experience success. Even as adults look back at their own educational experience, they remember most fondly the teachers that both pushed and encouraged them. They hopefully wonder, "Would

Coach Wallace be proud of me?" or "Does Ms. Shipper still remember me?"

To this day, when most of us reflect on our school experience, we still care about what our favorite teachers would think, wish we could tell them how we turned out, and share just how much we appreciate them now. Those were the teachers that Recognized our success, Reinforced our efforts, celebrated those small incremental victories with us, and were always on our side.

Finally, high quality, high volume, authentic, academic Recognition and Reinforcement is a *fundamental* component of a healthy, nurturing classroom culture and climate. In education systems, Culture, as defined by Dr. James Davis, is the sum of the policies, processes, practices, actions, and beliefs of the *adults* (administrators, educators, and support staff) in the school. This is true at the macro-level (district), meso-level (school), and micro-level (classroom). Climate is the positive or negative impact that the Culture—which is adult created and adult driven—has on *students*.[10]

In other words, Climate is the direct product of Culture. This understanding is paradigm-shifting and action focused. As adults and educators, we are neither blessed nor cursed by predestined school culture and climate. We are the architects, builders, and operators of it. If the adults on a campus want Climate to improve, there are two direct and concrete options. One, quit doing the things that have a negative impact on students. Two, do more things that have a positive impact on students. The teacher (adult) practice of increasing the frequency of Recognition and Reinforcement provided in class to every student directly improves classroom culture. The measurable positive effect of this practice on students directly improves classroom climate.

---

[10] School district leadership planning session, circa 2011.

As stated previously, many teachers believe they use Recognition and Reinforcement much more often than they do. This is because they miscategorize positive talk as Recognition and Reinforcement. It should now be clear to the reader the distinction between the two. But there are teachers that remain skeptical despite the education research supporting the practice and the observable success of teachers who purposefully use the practice. What is interesting is that when these teachers are interviewed, they can see the value of using recognition and reinforcement to improve student *behavior*. In fact, behavioral recognition and reinforcement is the cornerstone practice of many of the nationally known and adopted student discipline and behavior management programs. These programs train teachers to provide positive recognition of appropriate behavior and effective reinforcement of improvement in student behavior. What the designers of these discipline and behavior management programs know is when effective recognition and reinforcement of appropriate and desirable student behaviors is used frequently and consistently over time, student behavior improves. And the deliberate incremental teaching, reinforcing, and recognizing of desirable student behaviors is significantly more effective than continuously punishing undesirable behaviors. Our question to those teachers is, "Why be skeptical of the practice in one area (academics) yet see the value of the practice in another (behavior)?"

In performance-based activities, such as athletics, band, choir, and others, it is plainly obvious that the more effort the performer puts forth over time results in improved performance. This is why successful coaches, band directors, music teachers, and the like are often intuitively good at behavior-based recognition and reinforcement. These coaches (*teachers*) not only monitor incremental growth and reward it, but they also constantly reinforce the effort required to succeed. Few student athletes enjoy long practices in the summer. It is the recognition and reinforcement provided by the coach that gets players to show up, break a sweat, work so hard they get blurred vision…and then do it again. It is the recognition and reinforcement provided by the band director that gets musicians to practice their instrument in the morning, at night, and on the weekend. Yes, the actual game and the performance might be fun and rewarding, but the fun and reward do not occur without considerable work and effort. And the quality of work and effort elicited is dependent on the skill of the performance teacher (*coach*).

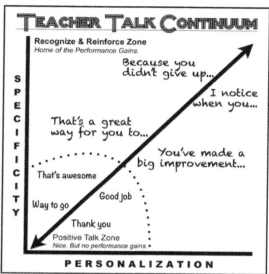

Figure 3.2

Essentially no one questions the power of recognition and reinforcement in other areas of our students' lives and development. The challenge is making the high quantity, high quality use of authentic, academic Recognition and Reinforcement not an exceptional instructional practice but a common one. First, as a profession, we must accept the fact that authentic, academic Recognition and Reinforcement is a significant high-yield instructional practice—a consensus ranks it Number Three in the ranking of the positive effect of individual instructional practices. It is the highest ranked instructional practice that, without exception, can be used in any setting, for any subject, with every student. It is solely the discretion of the teacher to use the practice...or not.

The commonsense approach to making high quantity, high quality implementation of academic Recognition and Reinforcement a common classroom practice is to train teachers on implementation and then support them through the process of awareness, moving them beyond implementation and into expertise. This is a leadership and coaching initiative, and it is a teacher enhanced practice initiative. Teachers, instructional coaches, and administrators should first recognize that there is a continuum of teacher talk. On this continuum, positive talk is at the bottom and Recognition and Reinforcement is at the top. See Figure 3.2.

Let us begin this discussion with the understanding that any teacher talk on this continuum is a good thing. This was true in the pre-pandemic classroom, and it is especially true in the post-pandemic classroom. The absolute worst case for teacher/student conversations on this continuum would be a room flooded with positive talk with no Recognition and Reinforcement. Let us be honest, this would be a pleasant classroom in which to learn. The only downside would be that the teacher would be tantalizingly close to turning a pleasant classroom into a pleasant, high-performing classroom.

At the lower end of the continuum is the positive talk zone. In this zone, teachers address larger groups of students: the whole class, Blue Group, Table 3, etc. Most commonly, the teacher is focused on a particular student but is talking at a large group and does not distinguish to whom they are talking. The teacher knows but the students do not. The actual positive statement is either general in nature and/or not clearly attached to a particular item, action, or situation. It is the positive statement you hear 100 times a day on a campus: "Class, good job."

As one moves up the continuum into the authentic Recognition and Reinforcement zone, the language becomes much more personal, direct, and concrete. Instead of directing comments to the larger group (class) the teacher uses a name (Watson). Or the teacher is near a student and makes direct eye contact so when they say, "you," the student knows that they are the one being addressed. There is also specificity to the statement, "Watson, your second draft is a big improvement over your first draft. Your effort and attention to detail is turning this into an excellent essay."

After this one brief conversation, this is what Watson now knows. He knows that his second draft is better than his first attempt. He knows his effort and attention to detail are the primary causes for his improved writing. He knows his teacher has noticed his writing. He knows that his teacher is impressed enough to talk to him directly. This makes him feel good, confident, and empowered. That, in a nutshell, is the performance enhancing power of authentic, academic Recognition and Reinforcement. Power that is not unleashed with "good job," no matter how much a teacher says it or how much they mistakenly believe that is the case.

The authors would like to draw attention to a statement (in Figure 3.2) towards the top of the continuum: "Because you did not give up." One of the most powerful conversations that can occur in a classroom is when a student receives an assignment back and the teacher notices that the student is obviously disappointed with their grade. Most teachers miss or ignore the student's reaction entirely. Of the teachers who do notice the reaction, many will see it, recognize that the disappointment is real, understand the emotion, but then move on. After all, the grade was lacking. However, this disappointed student can easily become demoralized and give up. Especially, when in this moment of despair, their teacher offers them...nothing. What the teacher should do every time students receive impersonal, negative information (see: low grade) is scan student reactions. If a student looks or acts negatively, circle back later in the class and check on them. The teacher can start the conversation by saying, "It looked like you were disappointed with your grade. Did you study/work hard/try?"

A student will usually respond in one of two general directions. The student could say, "Yes. I studied/worked/tried really hard and still did bad." This is good information that the teacher can immediately use. The teacher should respond with something like, "It's good that you studied/worked hard/tried. It may not feel like it made a difference, but think how much worse your grade could have been if you hadn't studied/worked/tried. Your *effort added* to your grade. It's not where you want to be right now, but you're *making progress. Don't quit*, keep working, and *we'll* get you to where you want to be." It is important for the teacher to point out to the student that there is a difference between what was earned and what they would have received without that effort.

The other initial response to the teacher's "did you study/work hard/try" question would be the student saying something along the lines of, "Well, I really didn't work that hard." Or the student could answer, "I forgot to study last night."

This is *not* the time for the teacher to chastise the student or tell them that they got what they deserved.[11] Instead, recognize the value of the information and respond in this way: "You know, some concepts take more work and more time to master than what we initially expect. It looks like this is one of those things for you. What are some things you can do next time to improve on this?"

This is an opportunity for the teacher to help the student problem solve. The teacher listens to the ideas the student has that could prevent the same situation from occurring in the future. The teacher may offer some suggestions for the student to consider. The teacher's purpose is to guide the student to a more effort and/or better time management solution.

---

[11] One of the authors had a high school teacher embarrass them in front of the class after admitting they forgot to study for a quiz (instead, they were studying for a test in another class that was administered on the same day). Whatever life lesson the teacher was trying to teach was lost, and instead the teacher made a focused and angry student enemy for the rest of the year. This author did barely enough to pass the class and made it a point to irritate the teacher daily, without ever actually crossing the line where a credible discipline case could be made to the assistant principal. This was a classic classroom case of lose/lose.

In both cases, instead of a demoralized student who is on the path to giving up, the teacher now has a student thinking about what they can do to have a little more success next time. The student picks up on the fact that this teacher is more in tune to them as an individual than other previous and current teachers. Their attitude about the teacher and the class moves in a more positive direction. The teacher is helping the student to begin to connect the dots between work, practice, effort, and eventual success. This is a connection that many students do not pick up on their own. The earlier in a student's life they make this effort-to-success connection and experience it, the greater their potential for success in school, work, and life becomes. Bottom line, teachers should want their students to leverage the understanding that even if they are not the most talented or fastest to master concepts, hard work and persistence can still win the day.

Consider the idea of "winning the day" and instilling that belief in *all* students. This is the idea that should drive the change in a typical teacher's practice. Authentic, academic Recognition and Reinforcement has a powerful effect on all students. This is an irrefutable fact. But the authors will argue that the effect is not equal. In actuality, the students who benefit the least from the practice receive it the most, and the students who would benefit from the practice the most actually receive it the least.

It has been observed that teachers and the education system overall do an adequate job of recognizing the most successful students. As educators, we assign As; give out gold stars; highlight the honor roll; treat the students in gifted classes and the top 10% like royalty; and elevate the Valedictorian and Salutatorian to king and queen status. But, let us be honest, the students who receive these kudos are already performing near the top of the range. When increased Recognition and Reinforcement increases the performance of these students, it is a good thing, but it is not a life-altering event. To be crystal clear, the authors are *not* saying to stop Recognizing and

Reinforcing the top performing students. We are saying, "Spread the wealth."

Educators should keep in mind that even though Recognition and Reinforcement improves the performance of all students, the significant, relevant improvement in performance is greatest with the students who are not already the top academic performers. A student improving their class average from a 94 to a 96 has not altered their education and life trajectory. But the student who raises their class average from a 67 to a 77 is passing and begins to develop a sense of hope. The student who raises their class average from an 83 to a 91 has an entirely new world of possibilities open for them.

In the typical classroom, the students who are not experiencing quick and easy success are more likely to become frustrated and their engagement in the education process wanes. With this reduction in academic engagement, less successful students find alternative means to pass the time. Even if this is only one student, the overall impact on the class is that the pace of both content coverage and learning is diminished, negatively impacting all students—top performers, average performers, and below average performers.

In the classroom where the teacher engages in the equitable use of academic Recognition and Reinforcement, students who would typically struggle and become discouraged and disengaged do not do so. Because of this, the pace of content coverage and learning is not diminished and begins to measurably increase in many cases. This benefits every student in the class—top performers, average performers, and below average performers. This is a flywheel effect created by the more equitable and strategic use of Recognition and Reinforcement—as more are benefitted, more benefit.[12] Moving

---

[12] Flywheel effect: Once a flywheel is moving, which takes some effort, the flywheel maintains continuous momentum even when the energy source is intermittent. Jim Collins, in the book *Good to Great* (2001), described the flywheel effect in organizations. A brief explanation is that as more little things are done

forward, the effect is magnified. This is most noticeable when the high volume Recognition and Reinforcement classroom is compared to a similar classroom where the practice is lacking, and more and more students become discouraged and slow down or quit working.

When managing and directing the chaotic, stressful environment that is the classroom, it is understandable why teachers conflate positive talk and Recognition and Reinforcement. The teacher's eyes see in one beat. Their mind registers in the next beat. Four beats later words are said, but by that time the teacher is responding to half a dozen other things that have occurred in the interim. Is it any wonder why most teachers never connect that what they meant to say and what they actually said are not the same? So, what should the conscientious teacher do to improve in this area?

First, for the teacher that is focused and task oriented (much of the profession), recognize that they do not actually use positive talk, much less Recognition and Reinforcement as much as they want to believe. When things are going well in the classroom, it is natural for the teacher to anticipate and mentally prepare for what is coming next. This causes them to miss the praiseworthy details that are happening in the moment. The unfortunate byproduct of this practice is when something eventually interrupts smooth and efficient learning operations, this event gets all the teacher's *negative* attention. The negative attention reinforces the one thing the teacher does not want to see. In a classroom with constant interruptions and a focus on negative events, the authors recommend that the teacher initially concentrate on flooding the room with positive talk. Granted, there is little to no measurable performance gain with positive talk. So why is this a first step recommendation? A high volume of classroom positive talk is the critical raw material that can eventually be forged into authentic, academic Recognition and Reinforcement.

---

correctly, momentum continues to build to the point where success become self-reinforcing and self-perpetuating.

Once the positive talk becomes an ingrained habit that is readily observable (a 30% observation frequency is a solid target), then work on turning positive talk statements into individual student focused complete sentences. Here is how this works. The teacher gets to the point of saying *good job, way to go, that's awesome, nice shirt, glad you're back,* etc., as a frequent component of their classroom communication. For example, the teacher recognizes that Kate is using her formula chart as she is working on a math problem. Positive talk requires the teacher to recognize this positive event (either behavioral or academic). The teacher sees the person who is engaged in or has done the positive thing. In this case, Kate. The teacher decides to comment on this event. The teacher says out loud, "Good job." Kate and the other students in the class do not know who, specifically, the teacher is talking to or what, specifically, constitutes the good job. The confusion occurs because the complete thought process in the teacher's head is not verbalized.

The enhanced habit, and hence the high-yield practice of Recognition and Reinforcement, works like this. The teacher recognizes that Kate is using her formula chart as she is working on a math problem. The teacher says exactly that. "Kate, good job using your formula chart." See Figure 3.3.

Kate, and any other student listening to the teacher, now knows that the teacher is talking to Kate—personalization. Kate, and the class, know that Kate is doing a good job. Kate, and the class, know that Kate using the formula chart is the good job—specificity. Same event, two different outcomes. A verbalized, incomplete sentence results in positive talk and no measurable performance bump. A verbalized, personalized, concrete, and complete sentence results in academic Reinforcement, and it sets the stage for continued use of the desired student practice and improved future performance.

If one were to refine this powerful form of teacher communication to a formula, it would be the individual student's name; followed by the specific observed process, activity, or result; followed by a positive statement or highlight. The secret is to not leave anything unsaid. Be specific, be positive, and repeat…a lot.

This better, more personalized, specific, and positive communication also works for adult recipients. Consider a principal who visits a teacher's classroom, observes for a while, and as they are leaving says to the teacher, "Good job."

This is a clear example of positive talk. Though this positive talk may reduce some of the stress the teacher may have experienced while being observed, it provides no meaningful information. The teacher does not know what specifically warranted the good job. Was it the student engagement, the working in the Power Zone, the classroom décor, or something else entirely? More useful to the teacher would be for the principal to say, "Ms. Tousant, student

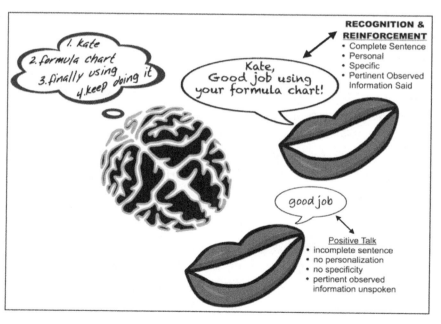

Figure 3.3

engagement really increased when you started Grading on the Fly. Good job."

Ms. Tousant now knows that the principal noticed her use of this better classroom practice and confirmed the positive impact the practice had on students as she was doing it. She feels good, and now there is a better than decent chance that she will use the practice again soon.

A quick way to significantly increase the amount of Recognition and Reinforcement provided in the classroom is for the teacher to begin *Grading on the Fly* (mentioned above). In addition to increasing the frequency of delivered Recognition and Reinforcement, this practice also allows the teacher to recapture a lot of time. The practice is simple to adopt, time efficient, instructionally effective, and students appreciate it.

The routine of most teachers, including the authors when they were in the classroom, is to get their students working on an assignment and then begin to informally monitor student understanding and progress. A student, David, asks the teacher for support and confirmation. The teacher, Ms. Martinez, visually *scans* the assignment from the beginning; *#1 – OK, #2 – OK, #3 – oops*. David has an issue with question #3. Ms. Martinez stops her review at question #3 and points out to David what he should do or correct to answer the question successfully. Ms. Martinez hands the assignment back to David and moves on to another student and points out what they should do or correct…standard classroom operating procedure.

Six minutes later, David asks for some additional support. Ms. Martinez visually *rescans* the assignment from the beginning; *#1 – OK, #2 – OK, #3 – OK, #4 – OK, #5 – OK, #6 - oops*. David now has an issue with question #6. Ms. Martinez stops her review at question #6 and points out to David what he should do or correct to answer the question successfully. Ms. Martinez hands the assignment back to

David and moves on to another student, most likely answering the same question.

Four minutes later, David asks for some additional support. Ms. Martinez visually *rescans* the assignment from the beginning; *#1 – OK, #2 – OK, #3 – OK, #4 – OK, #5 – OK, #6 – OK, #7 – OK, #8 - oops.* David now has an issue with question #8. Ms. Martinez stops her review at question #8 and points out to David what he should do or correct to answer the question successfully. Ms. Martinez hands the assignment back to David and moves on to another student.

Seven minutes later, Ms. Martinez collects all the assignments. Later that night, Ms. Martinez is home and spends a couple of hours grading all the assignments from the day. Assignments that she visually scanned and rescanned multiple times throughout the day. Again, standard operating procedure. But what if Ms. Martinez did the following instead?

Ms. Martinez gets her students working on the day's assignment; s*he grabs her grading pen* and starts moving through the room, informally monitoring student understanding and progress. David asks for support and confirmation. Ms. Martinez *scans* the assignment from the beginning, *leaving a record of her review;* #1 – √, #2 – √, #3 – oops. David has an issue with question #3. Ms. Martinez stops her review at question #3 and points out to David what he should do or correct to answer the question successfully. Ms. Martinez hands the assignment back to David and moves on to another student...*enhanced* classroom operating procedure.

Six minutes later, David asks for some additional support. Ms. Martinez visually *scans* the assignment from question #3, because she left a record that questions #1 and #2 are correct. She *leaves a record of the additional correct questions* she is scanning, #3 – √, #4 – √, #5 – √, #6 – oops. David now has an issue with question #6. Ms. Martinez stops her review at question #6 and points out to David what he should do or correct to answer the question successfully. Ms.

Martinez hands the assignment back to David and moves on to another student.

Four minutes later, David asks for some additional support. Ms. Martinez visually *scans* the assignment from question #6 because she had left a record that questions #1 through #5 are correct. She *leaves a record of the additional correct questions* she is scanning, #6 – √, #7 – √, #8 – oops. David now has an issue with question #8. Ms. Martinez stops her review at question #8 and points out to David what he should do or correct to answer the question successfully. Ms. Martinez hands the assignment back to David and moves on to another student.

Seven minutes later, Ms. Martinez collects all the *partially graded* assignments. At the end of the school day before she goes home, she quickly completes the assignment grading because most of the work was done during class as students were working. Ms. Martinez has recaptured a lot of personal time. This is a win for Ms. Martinez. But what about her students?

As Ms. Martinez is Grading on the Fly, she is providing students with real time, authentic, academic Recognition and Reinforcement. The first time she scans the assignment while standing next to the student, she makes a big checkmark next to each correct answer. Ms. Martinez is providing immediate Recognition of academic success. Each additional time she and the student scan the assignment, making additional big checkmarks next to the growing body of correct answers, Ms. Martinez is providing immediate Recognition of academic growth.

What about the incorrect answers? As the reader picks up in the above examples, as Ms. Martinez is Grading on the Fly, she does not put a big **X** next to an incorrect answer. Instead, she stops her review. At that point, she quickly confers with the student, addressing misunderstandings and mistakes. More importantly, she encourages the student to correct the work and not quit. She is now providing immediate Reinforcement of academic effort.

What also makes Grading on the Fly such a powerful classroom practice is that it ensures that the teacher checks on every student in the room. Every student needs monitoring and/or support while working on an assignment. The teacher has a vested interest in partially grading every assignment during the class period. The overlap of student need and teacher vested interest ensures that even the student hiding in the far reaches of the room, trying to avoid academic work, is checked on regularly. These are the students most in need of Recognition and Reinforcement yet receive it the least in typical classrooms. When these students are fortunate enough to find themselves assigned to a teacher who Grades on the Fly, both the amount of work these students produce and the quality of that work improves.

Another method teachers use to significantly increase the quantity of academic Recognition and Reinforcement provided in the classroom is the Scavenger Hunt strategy. With a Recognition and Reinforcement Scavenger Hunt, the teacher pre-selects the academic behavior, process, or action that they want to encourage and then purposefully focuses on that specific look-for. This could be almost anything. In English Language Arts and Reading (ELAR), the teacher might focus on catching students re-reading the passage or referring to a dictionary. In other subjects, the teacher could be looking for students using a formula chart or timeline, referring to their class notes, or any other value adding academic practice or activity that the teacher wants to emphasize. Then, whenever the teacher sees any student engaged in the targeted activity/behavior, the teacher reinforces that student, personally and specifically.

The Recognition and Reinforcement Scavenger Hunt is a very effective way to transform a classroom that is overrun with negative student academic practices and behaviors. By pre-selecting one or two positive things the teacher is most likely to observe during class, and then immediately Recognizing and Reinforcing those things as they occur, the teacher can quickly begin to turn things around. For example, if students arriving late to class is a widespread behavior, instead of providing late students with a lot of negative attention, Recognize and Reinforce the students who arrive to class on time. In a class where students only want to show the answer to the question, the teacher can deliberately Recognize and Reinforce the students who show all their work. In short, students engage in and replicate the behaviors that receive the most teacher attention. A Recognition and Reinforcement Scavenger Hunt capitalizes on this fact.

In conclusion, high-volume, authentic, academic Recognition and Reinforcement is a force multiplier. Figure 3.4 demonstrates this effect. Two similar students, in the classrooms of two different teachers, are taking the same course. Teacher One delivers a high volume of authentic, academic Recognition and Reinforcement to all students. Teacher Two is a typical teacher. See previously shared Figure 3.1.

On the first quiz administered in the semester, both students perform at the same level, earning a 72. Teacher One notices the disappointed reaction of their student and has a Reinforcing conversation about continuing to work hard and the improvement the student can expect. Teacher Two does not have a conversation with their student.

On the second quiz, Teacher One's student gets one more question correct. Teacher One provides their student with authentic Recognition of academic growth and continually Reinforces the student's effort. Teacher Two does not have these brief conversations with their student.

This pattern continues in both classrooms, with Teacher One's student improving slightly from quiz to quiz, and Teacher

Two's student becoming more and more discouraged. On the last quiz (Quiz 5), Teacher One's student scores a 92. By comparison, Teacher Two's student scores a 48.

Two students begin the semester performing at the same level. Two teachers teach the same subject, essentially the same way. Except one teacher is exceptional at providing authentic, academic Recognition and Reinforcement, and the other teacher is not. One student reaps the benefits of personalized Recognition and Reinforcement. The other student suffers the *devastation of lost hope*. Two similar students, same course, same difficulty level, yet two totally different outcomes.

Recognition and Reinforcement in the Remote Classroom

In a virtual instructional setting, academic Recognition and Reinforcement is arguably more important than in a face-to-face instructional setting. In a face-to-face setting, the energy of the class and/or the personality of the teacher can keep students focused and engaged, neither of which translate directly through a screen. Virtual

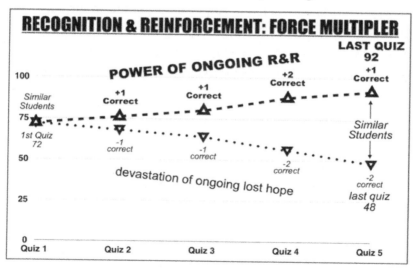

Figure 3.4

Recognition and Reinforcement may seem challenging, but a number of practical strategies were identified and used when virtual instruction became the norm during the pandemic.

The essence of Recognition and Reinforcement is personal and specific *communication* between teacher and student about the student's growth, success, or effort. Individual student breakout rooms and/or chat sessions are great opportunities for a teacher to provide a student with authentic, academic Recognition and Reinforcement. Teachers who work in a remote environment have reported it is much easier to connect with students and provide Recognition and Reinforcement in individual student sessions, with all the typical distractions of a face-to-face classroom absent. In addition to this, the ever-present ticking clock in face-to-face classrooms is not as oppressive in many virtual settings. This provides the teacher more opportunities and more flexible time windows to meet briefly, but purposefully, with students.

To keep students engaged and working, the authors suggest the teacher implement a Recognition and Reinforcement "grab bag" strategy.[13] As one would surmise, there are a variety of items in the grab bag. All students do not respond to all the items, but every student responds to some items. The secret is to use a variety of Recognition and Reinforcement methods or vehicles at high frequency, allowing each student a chance to experience the thing or things that meet their needs and personality.

Let us start with the chat box. If one is available, teachers should use the chat box feature whenever it is appropriate. As is the case in verbal communication, the teacher should write in complete, concrete sentences. Use the student's name and address the specific thing being Recognized and Reinforced. Many students find the

---

[13] Grab bag: An assortment of various items. In this context, the teacher identifies an assortment of Recognition and Reinforcement options that can be implemented quickly and regularly that enhance student engagement and effort in the instructional activity.

written teacher message more tangible, meaningful, and valuable than a verbal comment.

Many teachers have had success by having students create a progress bar at the top of their assignment. Students draw a rectangle at the top of the assignment page. The teacher instructs the students to divide the rectangle into quarters. When a student completes a fourth of the assignment, they get to fill in the first quarter of their progress bar. As they continue to work, they continue to fill in the bar. By doing so, the student is visually Recognized for their academic progress and visually Reinforced to continue working. With students who have a difficult time beginning or completing an assignment, the progress bar can be an effective motivation tool.

When working in a virtual instructional environment, teachers are encouraged to use all the embedded Recognition and Reinforcement tools available to them. Flood the virtual classroom with positive emojis, thumbs ups, smiley faces, likes, virtual post-it notes, etc. The competition for student attention when participating in virtual learning is fierce. High volume, teacher provided Recognition and Reinforcement is the most powerful tool to keep student eyeballs and attention focused on the teacher and their instruction. Providing students with personal and specific Recognition and Reinforcement builds motivation, trust, relationships, loyalty, culture, and climate, regardless of the distance. The more Recognition and Reinforcement, the stronger the bond between student and teacher, which significantly impacts student learning.

4 FREQUENT, SMALL GROUP, PURPOSEFUL TALK ABOUT THE LEARNING

The amount and quality of student talk in classrooms is tied directly to student achievement according to an abundance of concurring research studies. The influential education researcher John Hattie is straightforward in his conclusion after analyzing research on teacher talk. He writes, "There needs to be less teacher-dominated talk and more student talk in order to produce the challenging academic instruction that today's education standards demand." Hattie's synthesis of studies on this topic found that teachers talk for 70% to 80% of class time on average.[14]

As educators, we are well aware of the benefits of engaging our students in conversations about what we want them to learn. Most teachers agree that when students spend more time talking about what they are learning, they are more involved, more interested, and better understand the topic. In spite of this awareness and agreement, the balance between teacher talk and student talk in the typical classroom continues to tilt dramatically towards teacher talk. At the campus level, the profession has inadequately addressed the challenges teachers face when using student talk. Additionally,

---

[14] Hattie, J (2012). *Visible Learning for Teachers: Maximizing Impact on Learning.* New York: Routledge.

from the instructional leadership level, practical and manageable ways to support teachers as they attempt to embed more student academic talk in their classrooms have either not been identified or have not been promoted.

The challenges facing teachers who are attempting to embed more student academic talk in their classrooms are significant. Getting students to talk is not hard; however, getting students to engage in academic conversation is more difficult than the normal student chatter that happens naturally about what happened yesterday in the cafeteria. Managing a frequent academic talk process in which most students participate most of the time is a rare feat for a teacher making hundreds of micro-decisions about what they will say/do next without specific training to act otherwise.

The list of legitimate implementation issues begins to grow quickly. Some students want to answer all questions and either purposefully or inadvertently dominate conversations in group settings. Some students hardly speak a word and would like it to stay that way. Many times, these quiet students are the ones that need more academic talk opportunities in order to build their vocabulary, communication skills, and deeper thinking capabilities.

The teacher may have one group of students who finish their talking assignment in 30 seconds while another group is just getting started. There is always the risk that the group that finishes quickly will move to off-topic conversations which then impacts the focus of other groups and the quality of their conversations. Sound familiar? This does not occur because teachers are not trying. They generally are trying or have tried. Nor does this occur because students are undisciplined, unprepared, or immature. Granted, some students may be all three of those things, but any or all three are not insurmountable. In fact, the more undisciplined, unprepared, or immature the students, the more they need to participate in frequent academic talk.

Frequent academic talk in the classroom is a product of preparation, support, and patience. Teachers have to prepare and develop the questions they will give students in the hope of generating meaningful academic talk. These questions need to be preplanned if they are to generate the thinking levels needed to deepen student understanding and also be interesting enough to engage student talk. These deep, engaging questions are much more difficult to create than the spur of the moment questions that test basic knowledge of facts.

Since writing the first edition of **The Fundamental 5** in 2011, the authors' professional focus has been on creating, implementing, and supporting practical classroom solutions in the areas of high-yield instructional practices such as student academic talk. Our niche is helping teachers quickly overcome the obstacles to better instruction that are prevalent in every classroom. Engage with us as we share the options and strategies that we use ourselves and those that we have seen work repeatedly in classrooms and schools across the nation.[15]

Frequent, Small Group, Purposeful Talk About the Learning (FSGPT) is **The Fundamental 5** teaching behavior designed to promote student talk about their learning. It contains built in components that neutralize many of the challenges teachers face when attempting to increase student talk. The structure of this teacher-initiated talking strategy functions like a training tool that readies students for academic conversations. Frequent, Small Group, Purposeful Talk About the Learning has the longest and yet most

---

[15] The authors present to and train thousands of educators every year. Most audiences are enthusiastic because they know us, have heard positive things about us, or sought us out. Some audiences are more guarded because their attendance is not voluntary. Over the years we have learned that the more difficult and/or distracted the audience, the more often we must use Frequent, Small Group, Purposeful Talk About the Learning in the presentation. We also know, as former classroom teachers and campus administrators, that even the toughest group of students on a campus is easier to engage and teach than a group of busy and stressed adults who would rather be somewhere else.

self-explanatory name of any of **The Fundamental 5** practices. There have actually been many complaints about the name being too much of a mouthful. So why was this name selected, and why are we choosing to keep it, even with the opportunity to change provided by writing this new, improved version of the original book?

The answer is easy. Each word of this name is too important to omit. The name denotes the distinct differences between the correct implementation of the practice and the many other types of student academic talk strategies. Let us look not only at the meaning behind each word in the practice's name but also at what makes each component of FSGPT so powerful.

Frequent reminds us that the attention span of school age students needs to be a factor when determining when and how many times students will talk. The actual length of time is based on the age and maturity of the student. The younger and less mature the child, the shorter their attention span. As the student ages and matures, their attention span lengthens.

Planning for and implementing a short student talk session is one of the best ways to quickly reset attention. Due to this, the authors recommend that teachers insert a FSGPT session into

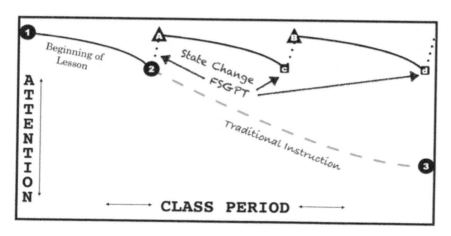

Figure 4.1

lectures, note taking sessions, or other activities where students have been focused for longer than their age appropriate attention span. No reset results in a drop off of student attention, and that drop off continues as class time passes. Figure 4.1 illustrates this phenomenon and the solution.

The start of the class is represented at Point 1. At the start of class, student attention is relatively high. The teacher begins instruction. If the teacher is talking or demonstrating, students pay attention at first, but then attention begins to wane. This occurs slowly until Point 2 is reached. Note, the length of time it takes to progress from Point 1 to Point 2 is a factor of both how long the teacher is talking and student age and maturity.

At Point 2, if the teacher is still teaching/demonstrating and recognizes the situation, there are two options. Most teachers opt to continue their teaching or demonstration. When the teacher does this, student attention continues to drop off in dramatic fashion, all the way down to Point 3. On the path from Point 2 to Point 3, the reality is that the teacher continues working as more and more students go on mental vacations. When this occurs, it is not the fault of the student. Instead, it is a significant and common instructional delivery error by the teacher.

Luckily for every teacher, there is the second option. With the second option, at Point 2 the teacher does not continue teaching. Instead, the teacher introduces a brief state change. A state change is simply a change in physical or mental state. For this state change, the authors recommend that the teacher have their students engage in a brief FSGPT session. After the FSGPT session, student attention is reset at or near the original level represented by Point A, and the teacher continues instruction to Point C.

At Point C, the teacher introduces another FSGPT session. At the conclusion of the session, student attention is again reset, now to the Point B level. The teacher continues this pattern up to the point that the teacher delivery of content concludes, and students begin to work on their assignments. The number of FSGPT sessions in the above example is determined by the total length of teacher led instructional time. As Figure 4.1 clearly shows, the teacher who harnesses the power of FSGPT is able to maintain significantly higher levels of student attention throughout the class period.

These FSGPT sessions are also important because they allow students to stop and process new information or skills, which makes it more likely the new information or skill will actually stick. Remember, the teacher is the expert in the class, especially when compared to the novice position a student holds when dealing with new content. Often what seems straightforward to the teacher overwhelms the novice learner. Processing new content, information, and skills by verbalizing it requires a student to connect this new information to the words and ideas already in the student's brain and allows better opportunities to retrieve it when needed. Allowing frequent talking opportunities not only resets a student's dwindling attention, but it also allows a teacher to maintain higher levels of student engagement throughout the lesson, and it significantly enhances understanding and retention. Delivering instruction in the way described may feel choppy to a teacher in the beginning, but it provides powerful boosts to the learner.

Small Group refers to group size, and by small the authors recommend groups of two students in the majority of cases. If there is an odd number of students in the class, then have one group of three students. Two students can easily talk face to face, on topic, and without difficulty. A pair of talking students is optimal because it is much more likely each student will contribute during the talk session. In a two-person group, it is easier for hesitant, quiet, or shy students to contribute to the conversation. A two-person group is less intimidating than a larger group for Limited English Proficient (LEP) students and students who struggle with content or background knowledge. All of this has the effect of maximizing the amount of talking time per student.

In a typical classroom, a teacher presents a question to the whole group and then works to get a couple of students to engage and respond. If no one responds, the teacher will answer the question for the class and move on. If more than three or four students want to respond, due to time constraints, the teacher is unable to give the additional students the opportunity.

Consider the simple math of classroom conversations. In a typical classroom of 24 students, if four students respond to a teacher's question, that represents 17% of the class (4/24 = 0.167). Add this fact to the reality that in most classrooms the students who volunteer to respond on a regular basis are a small subset of the overall class. A generous estimate would be that in a typical class less than 40% of students engage in academic talk on a semi-regular basis, and less than 20% of students engage in academic talk during a given opportunity.

Compare this to a class where the teacher embeds multiple FSGPT sessions in every lesson. In this class, all 24 students consider the question or prompt, and then every student talks to their partner. In the worst case scenario, only one partner talks and the other listens. This would represent 50% of the students engaged in academic talk (12/24 = 0.5). In reality, each student in the pair takes advantage of the opportunity to talk. This means that close to 100% of students in the class engage in multiple, quick academic conversations during every lesson.

It is the Small Group element of FSGPT that engages ALL students in academic conversations more frequently. From the above examples, up to *100%* of students engaged in frequent academic conversations. 100% of students is greater than the 17% of students engaged in semi-frequent academic conversations in a typical classroom (100% > 17%). The math is clear and formidable.

It must be noted that this high engagement rate does not happen immediately. Class routines and expectations have to be established, and student comfort, confidence, and competence have to be built over the course of a few weeks. For example, when first adopting the fundamental practice of FSGPT in a class, the teacher may designate A and B partners. Then, when releasing students to talk, they give the instruction, "This time, B partners start the conversation, and then the A partners can respond."

Purposeful describes the instructional intent and focus of the student conversation. Purposeful is completely controlled by the teacher, who provides students with a seed question or talk topic that drives their conversations. This talking prompt, in order to meet the *purposeful* standard, is specifically designed to increase understanding, promote connections, and/or extend student thinking. The prompt must be open-ended enough that students have something to talk about yet focused enough to keep almost all students on topic.

Purposeful also represents the timing of the talk session. The teacher stops and asks the purposeful question at the time in the lesson where student attention is about to wane and/or when it is important for them to put important information, ideas, or examples into their own words. The right prompt when *asked too late* is not as

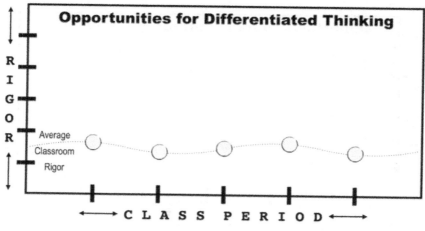

Figure 4.2

purposeful. *A weak prompt* asked at the right time is not purposeful. The teacher makes this quick talk purposeful when they insert a Purposeful Talk prompt at the right position(s) in the lesson cycle. The teacher makes the talk purposeful when they ask students to think about the content they are learning. Purposeful is a powerful component of FSGPT because of what it provides for ALL students. Purposeful Talk provides ALL students the opportunity to build connections and understanding more rapidly. Purposeful Talk provides ALL students opportunities to use content vocabulary in context. Purposeful Talk allows the teacher to purposefully spike and manage instructional rigor throughout the lesson for ALL students. Purposeful Talk provides the teacher with an authentic process for differentiation during the lesson that includes immediate feedback on how students are learning. Consider Figure 4.2.

This figure illustrates average levels of student cognition throughout the class period in the typical classroom. The thin dotted line shows that the average cognition level of the class bounces between remembering and understanding throughout the period. This is neither good nor bad. It is typical. The light grey circles represent *opportunities* for Purposeful Talk (PT). In the typical classroom, these missed opportunities are the primary reason student

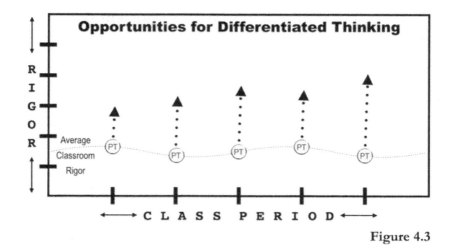

Figure 4.3

cognition levels remain consistent, day after day, semester after semester, and year after year.

Figure 4.3 illustrates the effect that multiple FSGPT sessions have on the cognition of the most academically able students in the classroom. In the example, the teacher embeds five FSGPT sessions in the lesson. The question prompt for the talk session is the same for each student. Equipped with this prompt and the opportunity to talk with their partner, the most able students begin to clarify their

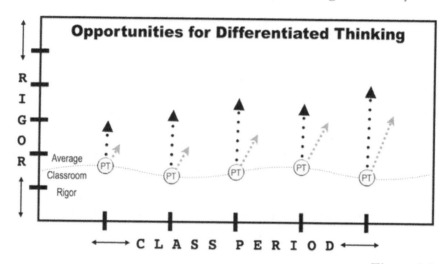

Figure 4.4

understanding, make connections, and think deeper about the presented content. With each opportunity to talk, their thinking improves, often to the analyzing level, even when the prompt was not developed at that level. The heavy black vectors represent this. When the talk session ends, the teacher continues to deliver content, and these students return to the remaining parts of the lesson better prepared to connect and understand at a deeper level.

Figure 4.4 illustrates the effect that the same FSGPT sessions, with the same prompts, have on the cognition of the typical students in the classroom. Equipped with the prompt and the opportunity to talk with their partner, typical students begin to clarify their understanding, make connections, and think deeper about the presented content. With each opportunity to talk, their thinking improves, often to the rigor level of the prompt. The grey vectors represent this. Though the thinking may not be as deep or robust as the thinking of their academically stronger peers (heavy black vectors), it is a significant enhancement over typical classroom cognition levels. When the talk session ends, the teacher continues to deliver content, and these students are more prepared to move forward.

Figure 4.5 illustrates the effect that the same FSGPT sessions, with the same prompts, have on the cognition of the less academically able and disengaged students in the classroom. Equipped with the prompt and the opportunity to talk with their partner, less academically able and disengaged students begin to pay attention and engage with the instruction. This is the first step towards being able to clarify their understanding, make connections, and think deeper about the presented content. With each opportunity to talk, their engagement and thinking improves. Even if this thinking never reaches the level of the prompt, it is an improvement over where their thinking began and would have remained without the academic talk opportunities. The light grey vectors represent this. Though the thinking may not be as deep or robust as the thinking of their academically stronger peers (heavy black vectors and grey vectors), it is a significant enhancement over their typical classroom cognition levels. When the talk session ends, the teacher continues to deliver content, and the operating cognition levels of these students begin to gravitate toward the overall classroom average.

When students are asked to think about the content they are learning, the thinking levels of a classroom of students will spread out all over the rigor charts (see Figure 4.5). More advanced students will quickly jump into analyzing and even evaluating cognition levels with a compare and contrast question. With the very same question, average students will likely reach the applying level of cognition while some may reach the analyzing level. Struggling students begin to reach the understanding level of cognition more often, with a stretch

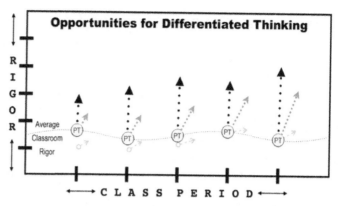

Figure 4.5

into the applying level becoming a possibility. The important thing for the teacher to realize is that a good thinking question will differentiate learning across the entire spectrum of the class, based on the ability of the student and their specific needs. This differentiated thinking does not require differentiated questions. It only requires the *opportunity*.

The most valuable outcome of differentiating with the use of a FSGPT thinking prompt is that all students grow in their ability to think no matter where they start based on background knowledge or prior achievement. Over the class period and throughout the school year, every student has multiple opportunities to practice and show growth in their thinking while learning the subject content. Purposeful is so critical to student learning while using FSGPT that later in this chapter we will provide guidance on creating Purposeful Talk prompts and implementing them effectively. Purposeful reminds every educator that the point of FSGPT is to lead students to deeper understanding of the content they need to learn. All students master content more quickly and at a higher level when they have numerous opportunities to verbalize both their connections and thinking. FSGPT is a time efficient and effective vehicle for driving *more* students to think *more* deeply *more* often.

Continuum of Types of Student Talk

If a teacher wants to improve the learning outcomes for every student in the class, then they should create a culture that promotes regular, purposeful student conversations about what they are learning. This chapter has introduced the reader to FSGPT and shared the better learning outcomes that the authors have both experienced and observed in classrooms across the nation. Purposeful Talk is critical for developing the deeper thinking by students that leads to deeper understanding about content. We challenge each teacher to start or improve on building this open culture of conversation in their classroom, where questions are not only welcomed but also solicited. Students are never cheating when they are explaining a concept or answering a how or why question for another student...except during a test.

There are so many different methods of generating student conversations about content that trying to list all of them would be a near endless task. Instead, we will generalize these talking strategies by placing them on a continuum—a continuum bound by the parameters of depth of thinking (rigor/student cognition) and instructional intent (required level of teacher planning and engagement to meet a specific learning goal). A reminder: any student academic talk is useful and should be encouraged and even celebrated, regardless of where it falls on the continuum. See Figure 4.6.

The bottom of the continuum is student academic talk of low rigor and low instructional intent. Think of this student academic talk as foundation building. This is where students build conversation skills, academic and working vocabulary, and a comfort level in talking to others. All occur while the student is talking to, being helped by, and helping their classmate. Rigor levels are generally at the remembering and understanding levels, and the talking strategies help students remember and gain understanding of knowledge and

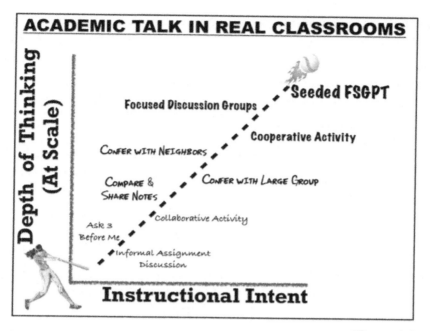

ACADEMIC TALK IN REAL CLASSROOMS

Depth of Thinking (At Scale)

Seeded FSGPT

Focused Discussion Groups

Cooperative Activity

Confer with Neighbors

Compare & Share Notes

Confer with Large Group

Collaborative Activity

Ask 3 Before Me

Informal Assignment Discussion

Instructional Intent

Figure 4.6

content skills. Talking strategies at this level include students informally working to complete a class assignment; students asking their neighbors for assistance or clarification before asking the teacher; and other collaborative activities where students can talk with each other while working but are responsible for completing their own assignment. These types of activities are commonly observed in classrooms, and using the softball/baseball analogy depicted in Figure 4.6, these are the instructional equivalent of hitting a single. Not flashy or overly exciting, but certainly better for the learner than working totally alone and/or waiting for the teacher to get to them when they need assistance.

Moving up the continuum, there are student conversations that occur while conferring with neighbors, sharing and comparing notes with a partner or small group, or conferring with a larger group on methods used to solve a problem. These strategies do take more time, structure, and possibly student training to be successful. However, at this level it is possible to get student cognition to applying and analyzing levels, especially if the lesson intent focuses more on comparing and contrasting, summarizing, or solving multi-step problems. Continuing the softball/baseball analogy, these instructional activities would be the equivalent of hitting doubles. Less common and more exciting than singles, and much more likely to produce an advantageous outcome.

Further up the continuum are instructional activities such as cooperative group activities, formal discussion opportunities like a Socratic seminar, or formal debates. These activities lend themselves to deeper analysis, evaluation, and synthesis levels of cognition. They do require teacher planning, management, time, and student preparation to be successful. When done successfully, multiple students can be observed inferring, justifying, evaluating, creating conclusions, and occasionally developing new and novel solutions. It is exciting. Surprisingly, these do not represent home runs. Instead, these are triples. A triple is a remarkable hit, and its potential for changing the outcome of the game is real, but triples are a rare event. Hitting a triple is the result of just the right combination of power, speed, and luck. In other words, teachers should appreciate the effect of these activities, and they should celebrate them when they occur. However, no teacher is planning for and managing a full Socratic seminar every day, and no rational instructional leader should have that expectation.

At the top of the academic talk continuum is Frequent, Small Group, Purposeful Talk About the Learning. The frequent use of FSGPT is like being able to hit a home run at will or on demand. A teacher who uses FSPGT with increasing frequency and quality is an All Star. FSGPT is a home run because it can be implemented immediately at any point in a lesson. Student cognition can be manipulated to a targeted level based on the rigor of the Purposeful Talk prompt. And most importantly, all students are expected to actively participate, meaning that ALL students benefit from the activity.

Rigor and instructional intent are balanced perfectly when purposefully designed by the All Star teacher. FSGPT can be used as a warm-up

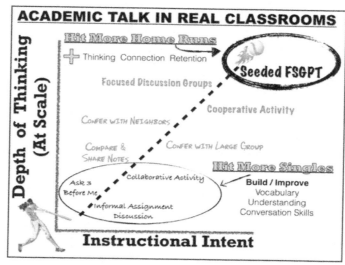

Figure 4.7

activity, a natural lesson transition, a perfect attention reset during a lecture or note taking session, a time for students to generate and answer each other's questions during guided and/or independent practice, and it is always an appropriate Lesson Closure activity.

FSGPT is a one-for-one replacement practice for the low rigor, whole-class-asked-one-student-answers questioning practice that is as common in classrooms as carbon dioxide—always present and too much of it will put you to sleep. Teachers need not worry about the doubles and triples of academic talk. If those activities work for some lessons, great. There is no reason to avoid them. There is also no reason to shoehorn them into lessons just for the sake of doing so. Instead, implement a two-pronged approach to increasing the quantity and quality of student academic talk in the classroom. First, hit a lot of singles. Build and cultivate the expectation that in the classroom students can always talk about content and the lesson. Academic conversations are always appropriate. Create an environment where students are comfortable conferring, supporting, and being assisted by their peers. If a classmate asks a question, answer it. If a classmate is confused, provide clarification. If a classmate is struggling, provide support. If a student needs support and the teacher is unavailable at that moment, anyone in the class can provide assistance.

This universal, informal, and near continuous student academic talk builds vocabulary, understanding, and conversation skills without significant teacher planning and management. It occurs because it is the natural byproduct of evolved classroom practice. The teacher builds the classroom culture of academic talk. Classroom climate improves as more students participate and become more confident and competent in their academic conversations.

Inserted into this environment of informal academic talk, the All Star teacher purposefully embeds two to five FSGPT sessions in every lesson. The All Star teacher purposefully increases student thinking about the content, strengthens connections to the content, and enhances content retention. In other words, the teacher hits multiple instructional home runs during every lesson, by design, AT WILL! See Figure 4.7.

Imagine the headlines: *The Streak Continues! Better Learning! Deeper Understanding! Robust, Broad Vocabularies! Campus Scholars!* What teacher (manager) would not want these headlines for their students (players)? PLAY BALL!

The Teacher as Time Lord

Frequent, Small Group, Purposeful Talk About the Learning is the *messiest* of **The Fundamental 5** practices, and the challenges mentioned earlier in this chapter are real. To confront these challenges head-on, the teacher must lean on the built in structures of FSGPT to implement and manage the practice effectively. If this practice was easy, every teacher would have their students do it all the time at a high level. However, our personal experience and thousands of classroom observations have taught us how to move this instructional practice from good in theory to even better in practice.

There are several important actions for the teacher to consider prior to the first attempt at FSGPT with students. Our Number 1 suggestion: Never forget that the teacher is the Time Lord.[16] The teacher tells students how long they have to talk, when to start talking, and when to stop talking. At the beginning of the year (or semester, or when the teacher first adopts the practice), set this expectation and build this routine. Initial FSGPT sessions do not require a rigorous prompt. The session should be very short, allowing 15 to 30 seconds for each student to reply. The reader may wonder, "How much can a student communicate in 15 seconds?"

Good question. The authors have thought long and hard about the answer. To build quality academic conversations, FSGPT is purposefully designed to focus on its built-in process. With a talking pair (Students A and B), *one student will talk and one student will listen.* Before letting the students talk, the teacher instructs the class that, for this session, Student A will respond to the talking prompt and Student B will politely listen. At this point, the teacher's modest instructional goals are for students to improve their conversation skills while discussing content *and* to learn to become better listeners. Even this early in the process, the teacher and the class experience a win.

Reconsider the initial microscopic time limit for this process to take place. If the conversation is flowing back and forth between the two students, 15 seconds is gone in a flash. If only one student is talking about an academic concept, (for example, a new vocabulary word) 15 seconds can seem like an eternity when your partner remains silent and listens. Since the teacher is in charge of time, adjust the time as needed. If most of the students respond in five seconds and then silence follows, the teacher tells the class that time

---

[16] In science fiction, a Time Lord is an extraterrestrial who controls and uses time travel technology. (*Dr. Who.* BBC One. 1963 – 2021. Television.) In the classroom, the teacher acts as a Time Lord when they purposefully manage time to maximize student engagement and optimize time spent on purposeful academic activities.

THE FUNDAMENTAL 5 REVISITED

is up. The students will not know that they did not get the entire 15 seconds. If most of the students are still going strong after 15 seconds, the teacher can extend time before stopping the conversation. Most students will not realize that they were taking longer than 15 seconds. Teachers should not make the mistake of waiting for every student in every group to run out of things to say. Students will never all finish at the same time. Early on, when building the routine, rotate who talks. One time Student A talks and Student B listens. The next time do the reverse. Keep it quick and remember: The students do not control time, and the timer does not control time. The teacher controls time. The process begins with the teacher assuming the role of Time Lord. The teacher selects and informs the students of the short amount of time (15 to 30 seconds) available for their conversations. Then, when the class hears the cue, one student talks while their partner listens.

Train, Practice, and Review Students

Students have to be taught how to be productive and successful in a FSGPT session. Depending on the class, this may take overt, direct teaching by the teacher and multiple practice opportunities for students before the sessions begin to meet the teacher's intent and expectations. The teacher should talk to students and explain why they will have hundreds of opportunities to talk quickly with a partner about what they are learning over the course of the year. It should be explained to students how much these quick discussions with a partner will help them retain what they need to remember in class and understand it better. Students should know that FSGPT will be a regular part of the class every day. It should be emphasized to students that the more they use FSGPT, the more normal it will feel, and the easier it will become to translate what they are learning into words.

Students also need to be reminded about how important listening is when participating in FSGPT. The class should *discuss what it means to be a good listener.* Mention, model, and practice the engaged listening basics such as eye contact, nodding, leaning in, and, of course, no interrupting/talking out of turn. Be sure to emphasize that the listener should be paying close attention because they could also be asked to paraphrase what their partner has said, answer the same prompt but clarify something or elaborate further, or respond in some other way. Building an entire class of better listeners is another positive attribute of the FSGPT process.

A valuable life skill students learn and practice regularly when participating in regular FSGPT sessions is developing *the ability to agree and disagree appropriately.* Regardless of their age, becoming comfortable with a variety of appropriate agreement and disagreement statements will help students be more successful in any interpersonal situation, be it at school, play, home, or life. This is especially true with disagreeing appropriately where defensive/negative emotions are quick to surface on either side if handled inappropriately. The authors have observed classrooms where the teacher has an anchor chart that lists ways to disagree and continue conversations with disagreement phrases like:

- That's a valid point, but…
- I don't share your opinion because…
- I understand where you are coming from, but…
- I disagree with you about this because…

This anchor chart becomes a living resource in the class as the teacher regularly updates the chart when students come up with other respectful things to say when they disagree and still continue the conversation. Polite and productive disagreement language is much harder for students (and adults) to master than agreement language. As students master it, the richness and diversity of classroom conversations begin to expand exponentially.

Another conversation skill that will need to be taught, modeled, and practiced is for students to be able to *extend the response of another student.* The teacher might have the FSGPT session begin with Student B answering the prompt and then after the allotted time Student A adds something that extends Student B's answer. For an accomplished, relaxed orator, this is not a difficult task. For a student new to purposeful interactive dialogue while navigating new content within a time constraint, the task can be overwhelming. As such, the teacher may want to share with their students the following extension phrases:

- Another way to interpret or say…
- An example of this would be…
- An important detail to add is…
- An alternative method could be to…
- The pros and/or cons of _____ are…
- _____ and _____are similar/different because…

Tracy Dennis, an educator in Texas and early master of the FSGPT process, created a resource she gives to every student. Students keep this resource on their desk and during FSGPT sessions they refer to it as needed. This resource? The Handheld Conversations card (see Figure 4.8). What Tracy realized before most of the profession is that Purposeful Talk is a daunting task, with variables and complexities that can quickly overwhelm students and shut down conversations. If the teacher provides students with a resource they can hold in their hands, the task becomes more doable, and the talk quickly becomes more purposeful.

It should be clear to the reader that students will need some training, practice, and time to learn the skills that make FSGPT consistently productive. As such, do not be discouraged by early setbacks. Even a "bad" FSGPT session resets student attention and allows them to better focus on the next segment of the lesson. Just engage in the process. With repetition and a teacher's guiding hand, all students (regardless of age, attitudes, and/or ability) quickly pick up the practices and skills

CONNECT	PROVE IT	REFLECT	I DON'T KNOW
✪ I remember...	✪ I choose ___ because...	✪ I now know...	✪ May I have some more time to think?
✪ In my experience...	✪ I think ___ proves that...	✪ Today I learned...	✪ Would you please repeat or explain...?
✪ This reminds me of...	✪ On page ___, it said...	✪ I am still wondering...	✪ May I ask a friend for help?
✪ One thing I've done before is...	✪ I think it might be ___ because...	✪ I'd like to know more about...	
Handheld Conversations	Created by Tracy Dennis	LeadYourSchool.com	(832) 477-5323
REPEAT	AGREE	DISAGREE	ADD ON
✪ I heard you say...	✪ I agree with ___ because...	✪ I disagree with ___ because...	✪ I would like to add...
✪ In other words, you believe...	✪ I like what you said because...	✪ I heard what you said, but I think...	✪ I also believe...
✪ Let me see if I've got this right, you are saying...	✪ I think you are right, because...	✪ I'm not sure I agree with ___ because...	✪ I was thinking...
			✪ My suggestion would be...

Figure 4.8

necessary to engage in a timely and purposeful academic dialogue. However, it is unfair to both teachers and students to expect students to immediately do well on something they have never been trained to do or previously experienced.

The authors constantly remind teachers new to FSGPT that it is a "direction" practice, not a "perfection" practice. During any specific FSGPT session, every student will not meet the teacher's desired expectation. But most students will. If most students meet most of the teacher's expectations most of the time, then the entire class moves in a forward direction at an accelerated pace. This is a win. At the conclusion of a FSGPT session, every student has had their attention reset. This is another win! Students learn how to navigate a conversation by listening while their partner speaks, then seamlessly switch roles with the ability to extend important and difficult conversations respectfully and effortlessly. This is an enormous social advantage for students. Not just in the classroom and in school, but also when they enter adult society and have to work with others. Win, WIN, **WIN!**

Teacher Decisions That Manage FSGPT

Frequent, Small Group, Purposeful Talk About the Learning is much more effective than other more informal and quick attempts at student talk because of its inherent structure and design. An effective FSGPT session is planned for by the teacher, initiated by the teacher, managed by the teacher, and used to meet specific instructional expectations. For students, FSGPT becomes an academic behavior, usually completed in 3 minutes or less, multiple times during every lesson. Students simply engage in the process. They start talking when the teacher tells them to start. They talk about a content aligned prompt that the teacher provides. They stop talking when the teacher tells them to stop. Finally, they receive Recognition and Reinforcement for their insights, contributions, and effort—which comes quickly and in abundance. Instruction and learning were occurring before the FSGPT session and continue after the FSGPT session. It does not look or feel like down time or time where students know their teacher is not that interested in how an activity turns out. The teacher is right in the middle of the action, managing and monitoring the session from the Power Zone.

Teacher management of FSGPT is active as opposed to passive, which is yet another reason why the practice is effective. The teacher decides *when and where* to insert FSGPT into their lesson. The teacher decides *how long* to give students to talk, generally 30 seconds to 3 minutes. The teacher decides *what question stem* to use. The teacher *assigns the talking partners* according to how their room is configured. Typical partner assignments are shoulder partners, across the table partners, aisle partners, and similar quick and easy options. What teachers who use the practice often have figured out is to assign talking partners that are already sitting close to each other. This speeds up the "getting situated" process and reduces student movement. Remember, students will talk to a partner frequently and class time is not unlimited, so fewer disruptions and improved time efficiency are assets the teacher should develop and protect.

How long a student has the same partner is up to the teacher. However, the authors would recommend a two to three-week window, especially for older students. Younger students could switch partners more frequently, if needed, to maintain engagement and mitigate conflicts that they may be too young to solve. This time frame is long enough to allow partners to get to know each other and build a partner dynamic. This is a good thing. The time frame is also not long enough for the partners to develop a superordinate/subordinate relationship. Often the easiest way to keep the talking partner process dynamic and provide a diverse pool of close proximity talking partners is to simply change the classroom seating arrangement every three weeks (or follow the progress report/report card cycle).

The teacher needs to decide what *cue will be used* to start and stop a FSGPT session. Some teachers use a noisemaker, some simply say "start" and "stop," and others do countdowns. It does not matter what cues a teacher selects. What matters is the *consistent* use of the cues. Each teacher and class is different, meaning the teacher has the discretion to determine what works best for their students. If a selected cue is ineffective, choose another, communicate it to the students, and keep talking.

The teacher decides what *reminders* the students need based on the upcoming talking prompt. The teacher might need to point out some useful phrases for agreeing/disagreeing or extending answers. The teacher might point out the vocabulary words on the board that students should attempt to use in their conversations.

When a FSGPT session does not meet the teacher's expectation (it happens), do not blame the students. Instead, the teacher should consider the decisions they did or did not make and the specific point where the teacher realized the session was not meeting their expectation. It is this level of reflection and problem solving that pushes the teacher through the learning curve faster and allows the class to enjoy the power of the practice sooner, rather than later or never. The inherent structure of FSGPT was developed specifically to reduce many of the conflicts teachers face when attempting to get students to talk more often in the classroom in a meaningful way. A teacher should stick with the structure presented in this chapter to avoid the often chaotic experience that student talk can bring and instead reap the benefits of increased learning that follows purposeful student talk.

A Basic FSGPT Session

The following is a basic template for a FSGPT session that a teacher new to the practice should use. The steps and directions are all included to provide a working image of the practice and to provide a concrete model to follow.

1. Announce to the class that they are about to engage in a quick Purposeful Talk session.
2. Remind students of their talking partner assignments. This could be a shoulder partner, table partner, etc. It is *not* recommended that students be allowed to pick their own partner. This takes too much time and introduces too many behavior variables to the classroom. Students should point to their talking partner. This physical action reminds students that they will only talk with their partner, and it allows the teacher to make a quick visual check to see if any partner adjustments need to be made. If there is an odd number of students, the teacher should make a group of three.
3. Remind students of the cues to start talking, switch talkers (if necessary), and stop talking.
4. Give students the Purposeful Talk prompt and give them five to ten seconds of think time.
5. Tell students which partner should talk first.

6. Tell students how long they have to talk. FSGPT sessions are between 15 seconds and 3 minutes long. Most sessions are generally between 30 seconds and 2 minutes. The length of time allotted to a FSGPT session is based on the following variables: student familiarity with the process; age of the student; maturity of the student; and familiarity with the concept being discussed. A FSGPT session during the first week of kindergarten would be no longer than 15 seconds. A FSGPT session in the second semester of Senior AP English could take as long as 3 minutes. There are no absolutes other than the teacher sets the time, and then the teacher assumes the role of Time Lord.

7. Move into the Power Zone and give students the start cue.

8. Monitor the discussion and call stop as time runs out. The teacher can adjust time as needed, subtracting or adding time. It is often helpful to give students a time update/warning: "You now have ten seconds to finish your thought."

9. If needed, or by design, give students the "switch talker" cue. Remind students how much time they have at this point. The teacher can have the second talker respond to the same prompt; elaborate, restate, clarify, or extend on the first talker response; or provide another content related prompt.

10. Maintain the illusion of accountability by moving through the Power Zone. Strategically check on students that are slow to start, hesitant to participate, and/or easily get off task.

11. At the end of the session, the teacher can immediately resume teaching without soliciting any responses, solicit responses from a group or groups, or address an issue that came up during the session. After some (not all)

sessions, many teachers provide students with a short amount of time to jot some quick notes. This is a power pairing of two fundamental practices, FSGPT and Critical Writing.

12. The teacher then micro-adjusts their instruction based on the formative information they have just gleaned from listening to the student conversations.

The Lever: Strategic Questioning

The Greek philosopher Socrates was once asked about the source of his talent as a teacher. He quickly replied that it was surely not in his accumulated knowledge but rather in continuing always to ask thoughtful,

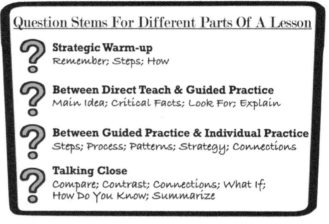

Figure 4.9

probing, and upending questions. As life-long educators and witnesses to the power of **The Fundamental 5**, the authors are in complete agreement with Socrates' assessment. In Frequent, Small Group, Purposeful Talk About the Learning, *strategic questioning* is the lever that begins to lift all thinking.

Strategically placing a question requiring the right kind of thinking (rigor) into the right place, purposefully *positions more students to succeed* as the lesson progresses. Strategic questioning is far removed from the spur of the moment questions that teachers use to get a reassuring head nod at the right moment. Strategic questions move the lesson from the beginning of the class to Lesson Closure. We have continued to study classrooms to determine what types of questions teachers ask that promote Purposeful Talk in different parts of the lesson cycle. Below we share what we have observed to help you as you select talking prompts that will enable your students to think (process content) at the requisite level necessary to navigate the lesson successfully. Make no mistake, there are some question stems that will fit in any part of a lesson, but there are others that just seem made to be a perfect fit in particular spots. See Figure 4.9.

Strategic Warm-Ups: Questions used at the beginning of the lesson should help students recall what they learned yesterday, remind students of previously learned material that is relevant to today's lesson, and remedy any discovered misconceptions or questions still unanswered. The teacher is indeed warming up student brains. Examples could include:

- What do you remember (or already know) about General Custer?

- List the steps we learned yesterday to find a common denominator.

- What part of yesterday's assignment seemed the hardest to you and why?

- How would you add a metaphor to this sentence?

The Transition Between Direct Teach and Guided Practice: Purposeful Talk questions used at this place in the lesson should focus on guiding students to successfully begin the content work that the teacher has identified or created. Question stems should contain words like *main idea, purpose, critical facts, look for,* and *explain.* Examples could include:

- What is the purpose of locating the topic sentence in a passage?

- What are the critical facts needed to solve this problem?

109

- Look for all the adjectives and adverbs in these sentences and explain how they clarify the situation for the reader.

The Transition Between Guided Practice and Independent Practice: Questions during this transition time should generate quick discussion that will focus understanding to the point where an individual student will be more likely to be successful when tackling the independent component of the assignment. Key question stem words often include *steps, explain, process, patterns, strategy,* and *connections.* Examples include:

- Explain to your partner how -7 is less than -4.
- How could you connect our study of brain function to change the way you study?
- What are the steps of the scientific method?
- Describe the process of how to elaborate.
- What are key strategies we have used to discover patterns in this data?
- What is a good question everyone should know the answer to before we begin our work?

Talking Close: Questions used to Close the Lesson are designed to provide proof of learning for today's lesson. Closing the Lesson with a purposeful thinking question is a significantly powerful retention strategy. At the end of the lesson the teacher wants as many students as possible to think deeply about and make connections to the content they were just taught. Compare/contrast and summarization questions are the *best* questions to use for Lesson Closure. Other powerful and effective closing prompts include:

- How did you know that answer B is the best choice?
- What would change if you substituted _____ for _____?
- What evidence supports your conclusion?

- What connects these ideas, characters, formulas, theories, etc.?

If the authors were working with you, in person, we would need to have a FSGPT session right now so you could process all of this great questioning information. Are you feeling a little overwhelmed? We would! More importantly, that overwhelmed feeling is exactly how your students feel almost every school day. Every day they have to process enormous amounts of rapid fire information from multiple content areas with little time for thinking, much less deep thinking.

After reading this far, you now know more of what to do and what not to do with your students as it relates to Purposeful Talk. We have shared strategies, practices, and tools that will assist in the successful implementation of the practice. What will separate the teacher who effectively utilizes FSGPT in their classroom from the one who does not is planning and preparation. Successful teachers build FSGPT into their lesson plans. This generally does not require any modification to the district or campus lesson plan format. To get the process started, Figure 4.10 is a simple form that many teachers have found helpful for both individual and team planning. The teacher decides at what point in the lesson they will embed a FSGPT session, either the beginning, middle, end, or multiple points. The teacher creates a Purposeful Talk prompt for the time(s) they selected. The teacher decides how long the FSGPT session should last (15 seconds to 3 minutes). Finally, the teacher decides what they should look or listen for while students are talking that will let the teacher determine the level of student understanding or lack thereof. This is the information the teacher will need to better micro-adjust their instruction during the course of the lesson.

Remember that generating academic conversations among students is not a one-time experiment. Instead, creating opportunities for students to talk about their learning is an ongoing process that should be cultivated and supported in a classroom. FSGPT is a vehicle that produces students who can navigate in a world that is changing faster than any educator can accurately predict.

When the authors walk into a classroom to observe a lesson, one of the first things they look for is who is doing the talking. Why is this the case? Because they know that the person doing the talking is doing the thinking. Language is how we think. Language is our operating system. Language is how we process information and remember. We are not trying to convince educators that student talk

Lesson Title: _____		Lesson Date: _____
Start Cue: _____	Switch Cue: _____	Stop Cue: _____
Warm-up (FSGPT Opportunity)	**Lesson Transition** (FSGPT Opportunity)	**Closure** (FSGPT Opportunity)
Prompt	When Does It Occur	Prompt
	Prompt	
Allotted Talk Time		Allotted Talk Time
	Allotted Talk Time	
Listen For / Look For		Listen For / Look For
	Listen For / Look For	

Figure 4.10

produces better learners. This is a fact. We are working to embed that fact into widespread instructional practice. No matter what subject or grade level taught, the delivery style, or activities chosen, the lesson needs a FSGPT session. FSGPT produces better learners. These better learners are students who know how to converse using important content vocabulary, can connect the pieces of a lesson together to understand content more deeply, and are better thinkers. For every teacher who wants to develop thinkers, it starts with Purposeful Talk.

Frequent, Small Group, Purposeful Talk About the Learning in the Remote Classroom

Frequent, Small Group, Purposeful Talk About the Learning can be challenging in a remote classroom with few options available in asynchronous settings or in synchronous settings without breakout room capabilities. As a work around, many teachers teaching in asynchronous settings schedule specific times for small groups of students to virtually meet with the teacher. During these virtual small group meetings, students are able to engage in quick Purposeful Talk sessions that allow them to deepen and extend their understanding of the content they consumed individually.

Communication can also be fostered through short connecting videos shared between students, or by using whiteboard and post-it note style communication tools that allow students to share their learning with each other. Giving students the opportunity to interact with each other in response to well thought out, purposeful, higher order thinking questions at regular intervals throughout the learning can be accomplished if planned for and if students are given the tools to be successful.

During synchronous instruction with breakout room capabilities, FSGPT becomes significantly easier to use and manage. Students can be intentionally or randomly paired/grouped and assigned to breakout rooms. While students are in the breakout rooms, many systems have a feature that allow the teacher (host) to circulate from room to room. If student breakout rooms are not an option, students can be given the opportunity to engage in remote setting FSGPT during teacher led/supported/monitored small group instruction time.

When small group sessions and breakout rooms are utilized in remote settings, students benefit from the opportunity to share their learning with other students and clarify their understanding.

Teaching and learning are enhanced when it is a communal activity. Children and adolescents need the opportunity to talk to one another about the learning and verbally communicate with their teachers.

Bottom line, if FSGPT opportunities are available, the teacher should use them, especially in synchronous instructional settings. Even if the quick student talk is not exactly purposeful, when students return from their assigned breakout rooms, their attention has been refreshed, and they are better able to focus on the next segment of delivered instruction. See Figure 4.1.

5 CRITICAL WRITING

Critical Writing, like other frequently used terms embedded in educational jargon, can take on so many different meanings that confusion often overshadows the effective use of this important member of **The Fundamental 5** teaching practices. To remove any confusion and restore clarity when describing this **Fundamental 5** practice, Critical Writing is defined as *writing designed for the specific purpose of thinking and making connections.* To meet critical thinking standards, the thinking level should be at the application/applying level of cognition or above.[17] Connections to almost anything already stored in one's brain are helpful, including previously learned knowledge or skills, personal experiences, relationships between similar things, ways to use this new skill or knowledge, or ways students see this concept already operating in their worldview. The more connections, the stronger the wiring that the brain builds so that new learning can be remembered and retrieved as needed.

Defined in this way, Critical Writing becomes the most powerful of all instructional strategies, as measured in terms of its

---

[17] Bloom's Taxonomy (1956): The levels of cognition listed from the lowest to highest – Knowledge; Comprehension; Application; Analysis; Synthesis; Evaluation. Bloom's Taxonomy (Revised 2001): The levels of cognitive process listed from the lowest to the highest – Remembering; Understanding; Applying; Analyzing; Evaluating; Creating.

impact on student learning. Writing critically benefits all students by improving memory, building vocabulary, refining communication skills, deepening thinking levels, making connections, and actively engaging students in processing the exorbitant amount of content information they receive daily. There is virtually total agreement among major educational research that more frequent use of Critical Writing would significantly improve student learning.

The Knowing/Doing Gap of Critical Writing

While Critical Writing is recognized as a powerful tool that assists teachers with their ceaseless desire to develop better learners, observation data from multiple reports, including the data bank used by the authors containing the results of over 250,000 classroom visits, show students in typical American classrooms are infrequently engaged in Critical Writing activities (4% to 6% of classroom observations). Teachers do contend they use Critical Writing more than the data reveals. But conversely, teachers also report they feel inadequately trained to teach writing and are already struggling to cover their required course content in the time they are allowed.

As former classroom teachers, the authors confess to having some of these same thoughts when various types of writing across the curriculum programs were added on top of their already crowded plates. With ever-increasing content requirements coupled with decreasing class time, these concerns are valid. Many teachers express the opinion that writing should only be taught in the English, Language Arts, and Reading (ELAR) classrooms where teachers are trained and competent in providing meaningful feedback and accurate evaluations of written work. This conflict between knowing that Critical Writing would indeed create better learners but not being able to overcome the obstacles needed to apply this powerful and fundamental instructional practice in all content areas has remained unresolved for too long. Fortunately, meaningful solutions enabling all teachers to increase Critical Writing opportunities for all students have emerged. Instead of viewing writing across the curriculum as a practice designed to simply produce more student writing, all teachers should view Critical Writing as one of the most powerful tools they can use to teach their curriculum.

This chapter will address the confusion and difficulties teachers face with incorporating Critical Writing in every classroom and content area. Engage with us because multiple suggestions and manageable options will be offered. These suggestions and options will require only slight adjustments in current knowledge and practice. The presented plan of action can significantly increase the frequency of Critical Writing in any classroom to the point where it will be demonstrated that *Critical Writing can be comfortably used at least one time, in every lesson, every day.* As you read, join with us to eliminate the all too prevalent Critical Writing knowing/doing gap by carefully considering how your district, school, or classroom can adjust current instructional practices and priorities to provide students with the most effective learning practice available—the frequent opportunity to write critically about the very content and skills students need to learn. In the post-pandemic education environment we are now in, best instructional practice is no longer a good suggestion. As a profession, we (teachers, instructional support professionals, and administrators) must display the discipline and persistence to implement the powerful, but underused, best practices we already know.

Rethinking Critical Writing

One source of ongoing confusion with Critical Writing emerges from the assumption of many educators that Critical Writing must be lengthy and polished. Polished, ready to publish writing brings to mind writing assignments such as multiple paragraph papers, expository essays, research papers, or critical literary analyses. These are all good examples of Critical Writing, but they all require considerable time to produce and the writing expertise to turn rough drafts into highly polished products. No wonder so many teachers believe Critical Writing falls out of the realm of possibility for most content areas other than ELAR and some advanced studies courses.

More confusion is added when teachers believe their students already use Critical Writing often in their classrooms, unaware that activities like copying presented material, free write journaling, and answering fill in the blank questions do not count as Critical Writing. These activities certainly have students putting their pens to the paper, but these writing examples are NOT Critical Writing because they do not generate the required thinking or connecting standards of Critical Writing. Allow us to continue to clear up confusion and investigate writing activities that will meet the thinking and connecting standards of Critical Writing and introduce less formal Critical Writing formats that take considerably less time to produce.

The relationship between the required amount of polish and the time it takes to complete a writing piece is important. The more polished writing pieces clearly take considerable time to produce. But the assumption that critical thinking can be expressed only in highly polished, lengthy articles of writing is not only misguided, it is detrimental to increasing Critical Writing in all classrooms. Focusing on the end product leads educators to misunderstand the power of the process of writing critically.

The process of writing critically transcribes the thinking going on in the learner's brain onto paper. Critical Writing converts subconscious thoughts and ideas into tangible evidence of one's thinking connected to what they know. Critical Writing considers and expands new ideas while searching one's brain for connections to other ideas already present. This process molds the unknown into relationship with the known. Putting focused thought onto paper is the purpose of Critical Writing. ELAR teachers across the nation report that one of the most difficult parts of teaching writing is creating the student skill set of transferring thoughts onto paper. This perspective opens our eyes to view Critical Writing in many different forms and varied lengths.

Beyond the polished, lengthy Critical Writing of conventional wisdom and ELAR classrooms, there are purposeful Critical Writing activities that lend themselves to other academic courses. But what if teachers embraced the idea of "thinking and connecting" writing and understood that formal writing mechanics are not a prerequisite for deeper connected thinking? For such a teacher, the seemingly mythical power of Critical Writing could be tapped daily, regardless of the grade level or content being taught.

As Figure 5.1 depicts, there is a continuum of Critical Writing activities, starting near the top of the continuum with the conventional wisdom of developing more polished and thus lengthy Critical Writing. But what about Critical Writing activities that require less polish and much less time? Do such Critical Writing activities exist? Yes. Critical Writing also includes such varied activities as short paragraphs, a few focused sentences, weighted lists, Venn diagrams,

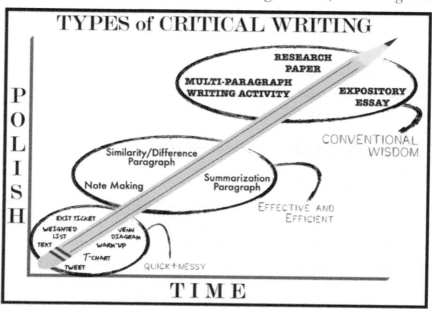

Figure 5.1

texts, warm-ups, note making (student generated), or modified exit tickets, as also illustrated on Figure 5.1.

These expanded Critical Writing examples, in addition to obviously shortening the length of writing expected, also move towards more informal formats. They encourage students to explore ideas and connections specific to the content without focusing on syntax, punctuation, and grammar. Using shorter, more informal writing with a focus on thinking and connecting encourages teachers to *use* writing, not *teach* it!

Teachers who utilize Critical Writing as an instructional strategy to teach subject area content redirect the purpose of writing from *across the curriculum* to writing to *learn the curriculum*. Critical Writing becomes a valuable teaching tool ensuring students will not only learn course content more thoroughly but will also improve their ability to write. ELAR teachers and writing experts insist that the more students write, the better writers, readers, and thinkers they become. They remind the profession that even polished pieces of writing start with a rough draft that serves the purpose of getting thoughts written down, organized, and connected. The more often students engage in this type of practice—writing for thinking and connecting—the greater the potential to develop large numbers of polished writers and students who retain greater amounts of important content knowledge.

Implementing Critical Quick Writes

Focusing on the thinking and connecting in Critical Writing instead of the grammar, punctuation, and structure, relieves the concerns of teachers who feel unequipped to teach writing. Reducing the length requirements of a Critical Writing assignment opens up this amazing teaching tool for more frequent use by all teachers in all content areas. One paragraph Critical Writing assignments are of immense value, especially when having students compare, contrast, and summarize. One to three sentences provide adequate length for students to quickly justify their thinking, whether they are defending why their choice is the best answer, supporting their opinion with facts or evidence, or explaining why they selected a particular set of core ideas as the most important things to understand from today's lesson. Using Venn diagrams, thinking maps,

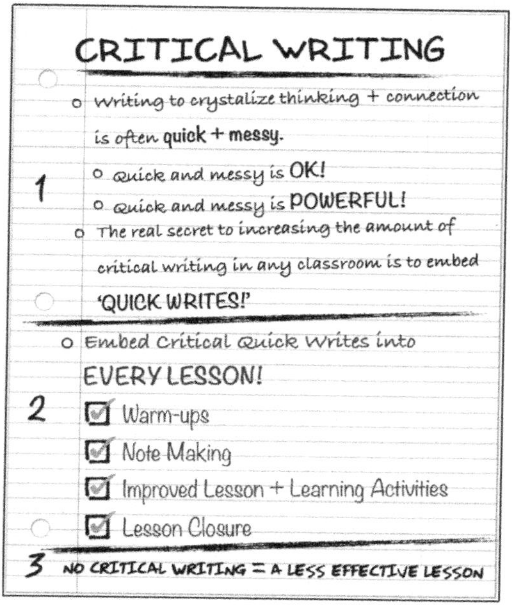

CRITICAL WRITING

1
- o Writing to crystalize thinking + connection is often **quick + messy.**
  - o *Quick and messy is* **OK!**
  - o *Quick and messy is* **POWERFUL!**
- o The real secret to increasing the amount of critical writing in any classroom is to embed 'QUICK WRITES!'

2
- o Embed Critical Quick Writes into **EVERY LESSON!**
  - ☑ Warm-ups
  - ☑ Note Making
  - ☑ Improved Lesson + Learning Activities
  - ☑ Lesson Closure

3 NO CRITICAL WRITING = A LESS EFFECTIVE LESSON

Figure 5.2

or other graphic organizers can easily become Critical Writing assignments if students generate and write their own entries onto these writing tools instead of copying answers the teacher has written down or stated.

Having students create a weighted list, answer a thought provoking question with a tweet, or respond to a rigorous prompt on an exit ticket can be very time efficient applications of Critical Writing.[18] Many adults worry about the type of writing that occurs in texts and tweets, but initial studies tend to suggest that students who text more frequently develop into better writers than those who

---

[18] Weighted list: A list of facts, attributes, items, etc., ordered by importance. To create a weighed list, a student must first remember the information. Second, the student must consider and compare the critical elements of the information. Based on the consideration and comparison of the elements, the student must assign a relative value to each individual component of the information in question. Finally, the student creates tangible proof of this deep but rapid thinking process on paper. From a cognitive standpoint, a student engaged in this quick Critical Writing activity would rapidly progress from knowledge level cognition to as high as evaluation level cognition.

never text.[19] These *critical quick writes* can often be completed in three-to-five minutes, which promotes using them often to engage students in any class.

An important thing for educators to remember is that there is a significant instructional difference between being attentive and being engaged. Writing about content topics, ideas, or skills forces a student to actively engage in processing information. Processing information is essential to deeper understanding and retention. Critical quick writes often produce messy writing, but the messy writing quickly produces decent to better thinking. The goal of using frequent critical quick writes is not to produce excellent pieces of writing but to increase how much students think about, understand, and learn the subject being taught. The good news is that even though writing mechanics is neither the focus nor intent of most critical quick writes, increased writing practice with focused thinking prompts supports the development of more polished writers over time. *It cannot be overemphasized how strongly the authors believe that teachers implementing frequent critical quick writes into every lesson, every day, at every grade level, and in every subject area is the most effective and efficient way to ensure better learning of content and create better thinkers and writers.*

The perfectionist (i.e., the typical teacher) has to embrace the understanding that writing to crystalize thinking and connection is often quick and messy. Quick and messy writing is not only okay, but also POWERFUL! This author was in the room as the core ideas for optimizing student outcomes (later known as The Foundation Trinity, see Figure 1.7) was drawn and labeled on the back of a napkin. The thinking and connection that quickly spills from the brain onto paper truly reveals the clarity present in the learner's brain on the topic or idea in the moment. This quick thinking dump reveals strong connections...or the lack of them. Strengths and weaknesses in background knowledge often present themselves along with old

---

[19] Center for Technology Implementation. (2014). *Using Texting to Promote Learning and Literacy.* Washington, D.C.: American Institutes for Research.

misconceptions. Obvious strengths and weaknesses will appear to both teacher and student. Figuring out these important factors quickly allows immediate and sometimes simple adjustments to instruction that happen naturally during the class period. This is much more impactful than remediating misunderstandings identified after an assignment, quiz, or test that is received by students days later.

The authors encourage every teacher to immediately begin to think about how to create solid, critical quick write prompts and where to embed them in normal classroom activities. Teachers who accept this challenge and significantly increase the amount of Critical Writing in their daily lesson activities will be on the way to becoming the great teacher described by author Doug Lemov: *"The most salient characteristic of a great teacher is their ability to quickly recognize the difference between 'I taught it,' and 'They learned it.'"*[20]

This author promised quick and manageable adjustments that will lead to using Critical Writing in the classroom every day. To this point, the intent has been to guide the reader to clarify their thinking about what constitutes Critical Writing. The definition of classroom writing was fine-tuned to specifically focus on writing for the purposes of thinking and connecting. It was pointed out that Critical Writing is a tool to better teach course content. Due to this subject area content focus, expertise in writing instruction and mechanics is not required to use the tool. It has been shared that while formal polished writing pieces are often examples of Critical Writing, such writing is not plausible across all content. Instead, what can be adopted across all content is the frequent use of an informal, quick writing style that encourages the use of multiple Critical Writing formats. Figure 5.1 showed a variety of Critical Writing formats including written paragraphs, sentences, note making, lists, graphic organizers, exit tickets, and, yes, even tweets. It was pointed out that

---

[20] Lemov, Doug. (2014). *Teach Like a Champion 2.0*. New York, NY: Wiley & Sons.

many of these critical quick writes could often be completed within a three-to-five minute time frame.

While these more informal critical quick writes generally produce quick and messy writings, it was explained that this was still beneficial to student learning and these writing products provide great informal, formative information to both teachers and students alike. These adjustments in our thinking about Critical Writing have opened up new possibilities to create better learners. With the elimination of several of the obstacles to using Critical Writing, let us now move forward in learning how to easily embed these critical quick writes into the lesson formats we already use. The reader should focus their thinking on their classroom or the classrooms on their campus or in their school district. The next section envisions the actual, enhanced implementation of Critical Writing. See Figure 5.2.

Embedding Critical Quick Writes into Normal Routines

In many classrooms, teachers use some sort of *warm-up activity* to get class started quickly and efficiently. Warm-ups are a great opportunity for students to complete a critical quick write that both enhances cognition and positions them to be more successful in today's lesson activities. There are a lot of good critical quick writing prompts that are appropriate for the beginning of class. The teacher could ask students to summarize three important things they understand from yesterday's lesson. Only a couple of minutes are required for most students to write a decent summary. This summary could be the first entry for notes that students will make during today's lesson. At the conclusion of the warm-up, have students share with a neighbor what they wrote. This gives every student a chance to hear another student's summary and compare it to what they have written.

In the transition between the warm-up and the direct instruction segment of the lesson, the teacher could call on a student to share one of their three important things while someone begins a class list that all students can see. The teacher should solicit several answers and then work with the class on which of the listed things they think should go into the summary. This activity will not only reveal how well students understand yesterday's lesson and what adjustments to make as the lesson progresses, but it also strengthens the students' ability to summarize. Later in the lesson, students could be asked to edit/correct their first summary to make sure all the important items reinforced in the lesson opening are present. Have students add this new summary to their notes.

Another good Critical Writing warm-up prompt is to have students write about which parts of the lesson activities from yesterday were the hardest/easiest and why. This critical quick write could be written on that very assignment (in the top margin or on the back of the page) since it is often still in student hands at this point. The teacher might also use the warm-up to teach students to write good questions relating to previously taught content. As one can see, there are several viable options for Critical Writing warm-ups that can be tailored to both student and instructional needs.

Another place to provide a good critical quick writing prompt would be in today's *class notes*. Even when the details of the day's content are so important and specific they must be copied directly (copying is not Critical Writing, but it is often necessary), stop at an appropriate point and ask students to write about how some new concept compares or differs from another concept they have previously learned. Another option could be to ask students to write a few short sentences using two to three new content vocabulary words that should be in today's notes. This would also be a great place to ask students to write a good question that assesses understanding of an important concept. Again, there are many options, but this short time taken to allow students to put their thinking into their own words provides them with the time necessary to process the material they are expected to learn. It is important to remember that if a note taking form is provided for students, there should be room on the form for students to generate some of their own connections and understandings in their own words. Leave an empty box or two as a reminder to give students a critical quick write that helps them process the significant volume of new content information they are exposed to daily.

Rare is a lesson where students do not complete some type of work or activity during the class time. Inserting a critical quick write *at the completion of a classroom learning activity* before transitioning to what comes next is pure instructional genius. Many students are seemingly more motivated to simply complete the work a teacher gives them rather than to learn from it. This happens with nearly every commonly observed type of student assignment. A great question prompt for students after completing a learning activity is to have them write an explanation of what they learned from doing the activity. If the activity involves practicing a skill, ask students to list the steps that should be followed and explain how or when they would use the skill. The depth and quality of the students' written responses help both teacher and students evaluate if the expectation of learning from the work assigned has been met. When the author used similar critical quick writes in her math classes, she was quickly able to determine what kinds of learning activities and classroom work were producing better student outcomes and which were not. Having students respond to these writing prompts right on the assignment they just completed also cements the expectation that students should learn something from each and every classroom activity.

Finally, the Lesson Closure is perhaps the most perfect place to use a critical quick write. A correctly implemented, appropriate Lesson Closure provides real time, formative evidence of student learning at the close of the lesson. Remember the 2 + 2 + 1 Lesson

Closure plan shared in Chapter 2. Summary prompts and similarity/difference prompts are the authors' recommended closing prompts because they naturally raise the thinking level of students to applying or above.

"I will explain the difference between a physical and a chemical reaction" is an excellent similarity/difference closing prompt for a science class. "I will summarize my solutions to the three biggest obstacles I face as I implement Critical Writing in my classroom" would be a powerful closing quick write for a lesson on implementing Critical Writing.

The author has had great success with providing students a note taking template with an empty box at the bottom of the page where students respond to the Critical Writing prompt for the Lesson Closure. What better place to have this evidence of learning recorded than at the conclusion of the student's own notes? The author has also used strips of paper, post-it notes, and note cards for students to write their response to the closing prompt. These are then collected as students exit the classroom. The benefit of this practice is two-fold. First, student accountability to participate in the lesson is increased. Second, and most important, the teacher is provided with an immediate assessment of whether students learned what the teacher attempted to teach and the relative success of the teaching method. This does not take as much time as one would initially believe. The teacher can thumb through a set of exit slips during the passing period while standing in the hallway outside their door as they wait for the next class of students to arrive.

Embedding critical quick write activities into normal classroom routines makes them increasingly easier to manage. Knowing that teachers have legitimate questions about where students should actually write their responses led the author to make the suggestions shared above. Teachers should keep their options open and have students engage in the particular critical quick write format that best meets the instructional needs of a lesson and works within the teacher's organizational and classroom management style. Critical Writing can occur on a note card, a strip of paper, a designed writing form that can be kept for a week or two, a post-it note, an individual white board, or even on the back of a napkin. More important than what the students will actually write on is the question of how does the teacher process and use the formative information provided via frequent critical quick writes.

Assessing Learning with Critical Quick Writes

The formative information provided by the frequent use of critical quick writes is significantly enhanced as the teacher becomes a master at the illusion of accountability. Learning how to provide individual accountability actions for these critical quick writes is essential in keeping students engaged and motivated. Students must believe that their teacher has a great interest in what they are writing. Fortunately, **The Fundamental 5** behaviors have given you multiple ideas for accomplishing this task without becoming overwhelmed with the thoughts of collecting or grading a significant volume of critical quick writes.

Step one is to maximize the amount of time the teacher is in the Power Zone while students are engaged in Critical Writing activities. The teacher should purposefully move throughout the room, specifically looking at student writing. Teachers who do this are able to quickly determine what students are and are not learning. Moving through the classroom and observing student writing as they are doing it encourages better participation and allows the teacher to reinforce the expectation that everyone writes. This intentional observation of Critical Writing in process increases the overall quality of responses. The teacher can ask a quick finishing student to elaborate more or provide a struggling student with a sentence stem to get them started. Pointing out a vocabulary word on the board suddenly reminds every student of that list of words, and the frequent suggestion that they use those words in their response increases the likelihood that they will. Simple approval documentation on student papers as they write (like checkmarks, smiley faces, or a positive rubber stamp image) indicates to the student that the teacher approves of their effort and/or understanding up to that point in their work. A friendly smile, a fist bump, or a thumbs-up signal goes a long way towards encouraging better writing outcomes.

The Fundamental 5 behavior of Recognition and Reinforcement embodies giving Recognition that addresses specific academic expectations being met. As such, when warranted, a teacher should add a quick comment about the thinking level of a student's response or the strong connections the student made to something the teacher had never considered. Provide a comment (in addition to a star stamp) to a student enjoying real academic improvement or to a student who is providing exceptional effort. The better a teacher becomes at supporting and informally monitoring students engaged in Critical Writing, the better student writing matches teacher expectations. The better the teacher is able to guide students to stay on track, the better the teacher becomes at creating more effective Critical Writing prompts, and the fewer days the teacher will experience student responses that are just plain bad (it happens to everyone).

The Fundamental 5 behavior of engaging students in Frequent, Small Group, Purposeful Talk provides teachers with another great accountability technique. Students can be asked to share their writing with a talking partner, a small group, or with the entire class when appropriate. A student can be asked to paraphrase what another student has written. Students can choose the best-written response from their small group and share that response with the class or another group. While students are working on their independent writing task, the teacher can facilitate conversations between a few individual students about their critical quick writes.

Over the course of just two or three days, the teacher can look at, provide an affirmation, and converse with each individual student about one of their recent critical quick writes. These ideas may sound simple and perhaps juvenile, but the authors have found them to be effective with students of all ages, in all subject areas, across the entire span of school settings. Student Critical Writing is so revealing of student learning that teachers new to the practice are amazed at how many times they are able to quickly and effortlessly adjust their instruction to correct a lack of understanding or misconceptions they just identified. There are some occasions where teachers may want to collect and formally grade a critical quick write, but it is not required for the vast majority of student Critical Writing. Just remember when either formally grading or giving informal feedback on a critical quick write response that spelling, grammar, punctuation, and/or sentence structure are not the focus. With critical quick writes the teacher should only be concerned with student thinking about content, making significant connections, explaining ideas, and making a good effort.

The authors worked with a high school that made rapid and significant progress with the overall quality of Critical Writing by implementing the following practice. Recognizing the power of Critical Writing, core content (ELAR, Math, Science, Social Studies) and core related elective teachers committed to using a written Close three times a week. Monday through Thursday, the teacher could decide if a talking or written Close would be used. If a written Close was selected, then any critical quick write format was acceptable. Friday was slightly different. Friday was always a written Close and the format was always a short paragraph (three to five sentences).

The question then became, how can a non-ELAR teacher quickly grade 175 paragraphs during the day? The solution was novel and genius. The novel part of the solution was the ELAR department developed a closing paragraph grading rubric for the campus that both teachers and students used. Every teacher could quickly scan a

---

Friday Writing Rubric

---

5 - The response demonstrates a clear understanding of the concept or process. Any writing mechanics issues are minor and minimal.

4 - The response demonstrates a clear understanding of the concept or process. Writing mechanics are informal or draft level quality.

3 - The response indicates the expected level of understanding of the concept or process. Explanations and/or connections meet lesson expectations.

2 - The response demonstrates effort. The response indicates an initial understanding of the problem or process.

1 - *The response demonstrates effort. The response does not indicate an understanding of the concept or process.*

0 - *No response / did not participate.*

The student can submit their **BEST** Friday writing, **FROM ANY CLASS,** to their English teacher for an **EXTRA GRADE.**

Figure 5.3

student's paragraph and give it a score of one to five based on the rubric. The score provided quick and meaningful feedback to students because they also knew the rubric criteria. The genius part of the solution was that the student then decided (with the help of the rubric) what was their best Critical Writing sample of the day. The student could then present that writing sample (regardless of subject area) to their ELAR teacher for an ELAR grade. Essentially, this was an extra credit grade the student could earn every week. With the adoption of this campus wide practice, Critical Writing became important to every student, which in turn rapidly transformed the campus from typical to exceptional, based on the comparison of state performance results among peer campuses. See Figure 5.3.

Thinking with Content Knowledge

Critical Writing focuses on generating critical thinking about the content students need to learn. The pressure teachers face to raise the thinking levels of students in their classroom is real. Just mentioning the word *rigor* creates a level of teacher anxiety about how to raise instructional rigor without leaving a significant number of students behind or in a constant state of struggle. In the same way the profession once erroneously believed that Critical Writing was the product of long, polished, formal pieces of writing, too many in the profession still erroneously believe that *rigor* and *hard* are the same thing. In theory, we know that this is not true, but our practice frequently tries to create rigorous thinking activities that both look hard and cannot possibly be completed during a typical class period. We also make the false assumptions that until students have learned and mastered "the basics," they are neither ready nor able to think rigorously. This ignores years of brain research that has specifically communicated to teachers that students learn information best when they are required to "use" it. Every teacher can immediately think of areas in their content where relevant applications are easy to find. Those same teachers have also experienced areas in their content that require the equivalent of a gymnastic freestanding backflip to draw attention away from their inability to even give examples of relevant applications.

While teachers seek applications to help students make learning relevant and worth the effort, our increased understanding of critical thinking skills opens up many new possibilities to consider as means to "use" knowledge. A significantly important way to use knowledge is to merge it into critical thinking skills. Students have to use knowledge when teachers ask them to summarize. A summary is impossible unless students concentrate on the components of important new ideas blended with prior knowledge and experiences. Students use knowledge when comparing and contrasting. They cannot even begin this thinking assignment without seeking to remember information about the topics to compare. And every time a teacher has a student recall a concept or idea, they have strengthened its presence in long-term memory. Decision making is weakened without recalling important conceptual knowledge needed to analyze choices and options. Attempts to explain how or why fall flat without remembering important facts. Interpreting maps, charts, tables, and data require both a command of content knowledge and the ability to think critically. Knowledge and thinking skills should not be isolated. Students learn by blending their knowledge into their thinking skills. The old adage *use it or lose it* aligns perfectly with brain compatible learning. Memory should be more accurately thought of as a muscle, not a storage vessel. Students assimilate knowledge faster when they use that knowledge to better think. Critical Writing is the instructional activity that makes all students think specifically about content, which in turn improves their ability to think regardless of content.

Critical Writing (the most effective and efficient vehicle to promote critical thinking) is bigger than just an instructional practice or activity. The post-pandemic teacher should understand that the critical thinking skills that are developed and honed while writing critically in their class are also real life skills that are necessary to survive and thrive in an increasingly complex and competitive world. A student who cannot summarize does not possess a requisite competency of a supervisory work role, from shift leader to CEO. The student who never masters the ability to compare and contrast will always be at greater risk of being someone's dupe. A student who does not have the opportunity to practice justifying their opinion or ideas is more likely to blindly accept the opinions and ideas of others. Do note that Critical Writing (and hence, critical thinking) is not a one-and-done activity. It is the high frequency use of and engagement in Critical Writing that is essential to provide enough practice to refine both the knowledge learned and the ability to think with it.

Absent an accurate window into the brain, teachers are often left to wonder about what kind of thinking is going on in a student's head. Teachers create an accurate window in the brains of their students when they provide frequent opportunities to write critically. As students write, they reveal the depth, breadth, and quality of their thinking in real time. There should be no question why the teacher who has and effectively uses this formative information has students who are measurably more successful than the teacher who does not have similar information. Even worse would be the teacher that has the information but elects not to use it.

Creating Powerful Critical Writing Prompts

Experience has taught us that creating quality Critical Writing prompts can cause a great deal of teacher stress. Teachers, already overwhelmed by too many different demands, do not need yet another one added to their plates. As such, the authors want to provide teachers with a good sample supply of quality, critical quick write prompts that are at the application level of cognition (or higher) and encourage connection making. The intent is to provide teachers, regardless of grade level or content, with solid Critical Writing prompts that can be used immediately and easily as they become more comfortable with the practice. The post-pandemic expectation is that an academic content teacher will create at least one Critical Writing opportunity in every lesson, every day.

Let us begin with three Critical Writing activities that simply cannot be used often enough. These three—Written Similarities and Differences, Written Summarization, and Note Making—have been recognized as the pinnacle of effective instruction since the publication of *Classroom Instruction That Works: Research-based Strategies for Increased Student Achievement.*[21] Released in 2001, the book provides an overview of the meta-analysis research of over 100 studies covering the effectiveness of instructional strategies. Numerous research studies since then have repeatedly confirmed the powerful impact of these strategies.

Written Similarities and Differences is the most powerful instructional practice. Using similarities and differences as a Critical Writing activity is a win/win for students and teachers. Assessment

---

[21] Marzano. R., J., Pickering, D., & Pollock, J., E., (2001). *Classroom Instruction That Works: Research-based Strategies for Increased Student Achievement.* Alexandria, VA: Association for Supervision and Curriculum Development.

tests at the state, national, college entrance, and work force entry levels all count on this thinking skill to reveal mastery of learned content in all subject areas. Identifying what is alike and different about important concepts requires good content knowledge and the ability to break each concept or idea into smaller pieces. Identifying similarities and differences is implicit in learning how to compare, and it is critical to classifying. The authors have witnessed measurable student performance growth in subject areas, grade levels, and entire schools that have used only similarities and differences prompts in their critical quick writes as Lesson Closures for up to a month at a time. Though this may seem excessive to some, after a month of focused writing, teachers were able to craft more nuanced, purposeful prompts, and the quality of student writing noticeably improved.

On one campus where the authors were supporting teachers, a first year science teacher produced the highest state test scores in the district. What is the one thing the rookie teacher did that the veteran teachers did not? For the 6-week period leading up to the state exams, that teacher Closed the Lesson by having students engage in a written similarities/differences Close. A teacher cannot go wrong with having students write using this thinking skill. Its impact on student achievement has been validated by research over and over.

Written Summarization is the second most powerful instructional practice. Written summarization is a thinking tool that improves student learning because it is a skill that enhances a student's ability to synthesize and organize information in a way that captures the main ideas and supporting details. A major divider of successful and unsuccessful students is the ability to determine what is important conceptually and what is considered as either minor or supporting details. Summarization is a skill that should be used as a Critical Writing prompt repeatedly because it requires frequent practice before a student can consistently produce a quality response. Summarization strengthens student vocabulary knowledge and skills because it is impossible to condense a lot of information without a command of academic content terms. In addition to being an important adult success skill, summarization enhances student cognition, often elevating it to the application and analysis levels.

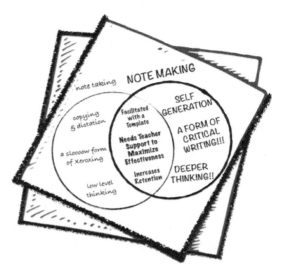

Figure 5.4

Note   Making differs from note taking, with most teachers being unaware of the distinction. See Figure 5.4. Note making requires students to write notes and make connections using their own words. Note taking is the verbatim, or near verbatim, copying of presented content, written or verbal. Both are useful instructional activities, but only note making registers as Critical Writing.

Often a lesson may require students to do both. Obviously, there is some information that students must know perfectly. But if a teacher has students engaged in a legitimate copying activity, they should also have students write something about what they copied in their own words. A quick summary or compare and contrast of important concepts would elevate the note taking to a Critical Writing activity, increasing student thinking and improving the effectiveness of the lesson. When students copy something exactly, it consumes their focus, making it difficult to process the information or connect the information in a way that makes it more meaningful. By giving students the quick opportunity to connect and write in their own words, the information is more rapidly assimilated and better understood.

The authors recommend that teachers adopt a standard note making form. Using a standardized note making template helps students organize thoughts into major categories. Students can be taught to quickly make a powerful and useful note making form on a sheet of their own paper. Have students draw a large rectangle covering most of the page and then divide the rectangle into quarters forming four equal writing boxes. Have them label these four boxes with major categories students should focus on during the lesson. Then have students draw a smaller rectangular box at the bottom of the page to use for the Lesson Closure writing box. See Figure 5.5.

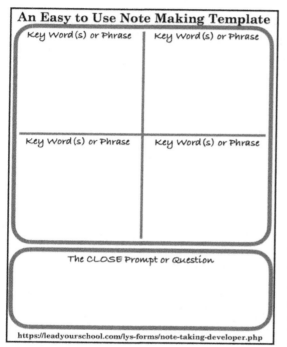

Figure 5.5

Once the note making form is completed, students have an easy and logical process to note important information, make connections, and organize their thoughts. Note making requires students to make lots of connections and decisions about what is important, and it then makes that new knowledge more tangible and retrievable when they write it down. The note making template shown in Figure 5.5 provides all students with a structure and process that positions them to make notes that are purposeful and useful in any setting.

When students are engaged in a note making activity, the teacher should stop on a regular basis and allow students to work in pairs comparing what each has included, or not included, in their notes. This allows students to edit, add, and/or correct their notes while processing this information verbally with a peer. The bottom line is that similarities/differences, summaries, and note making are always an option when creating Critical Writing opportunities in a lesson. Teachers should use these three Critical Writing activities as often as possible.

The following is a list of Critical Writing Power Prompts. The regular use of these prompts drive improved student outcomes by positioning students to think about content through writing. The bold statements are prompt stems. The bulleted items are examples of how the stem could be completed by the teacher.

Explain how...

- You solved this equation.
- Technology has helped or harmed education.
- You could measure the earth's circumference.
- The author revealed that the hero is afraid.

Explain why...

- Answer choice B is the best, correct answer.
- The status quo might need to be challenged.
- The Roman Empire was overthrown.
- You must have the same denominator before you can add fractions.

What if...

- You could change one thing in this story, what would it be, and why?
- The length of the side of a square doubled in size, by how much would the area of that square change?

- Everyone immediately changed to solar energy in our state, what do you think would happen?

Give examples...

- Of deductive and inductive reasoning.
- Of countries that contain tropical rain forests.
- Of objects in your home that are good conductors of heat.
- Of items that are measured in fractions.
- Of the author's use of metaphors.

Give evidence...

- That wind turbines negatively impact the environment.
- That the author wants the reader to try more adventurous hobbies.
- That the answer must be a negative number.

Justify or defend...

- Your choice of political party.
- Your opinion about control of free speech on social media platforms.
- Your answer to the stated problem.

How do you know...

- That *quickly* is an adjective in this sentence.
- To use addition or subtraction to solve this problem.
- That this character is shy.
- Whether to start this word with a capital letter or not.
- What the word *flexible* means in this paragraph.

Give interpretations...

- From the information in this frequency table, what is the best day of the month to sell pencils to 6th graders?
- According to this graph, what is charged per hour to rent an electric scooter?
- From this advertisement, what can you infer about the housing market in Japan?
- What is this cartoon implying about China's control over U.S. technology?

Explain the purpose...

- Of the wiring pattern in this circuit.
- Of reducing a fraction to its lowest terms.
- Of learning three ways to create tone in your writing.
- Of studying world cultures in geography.

What is another way...

- To add these numbers quickly in your head.
- To resolve the conflict in this story.
- To explain your idea.
- To use this formula.
- To demonstrate what you know.

The above prompts, along with similarities/differences, summarization, and note making, provide every teacher with a versatile and powerful set of quick Critical Writing options (see Figure 5.6). As teachers become more comfortable and students become more proficient in writing critically, the teacher is encouraged to create some Critical Writing prompts of their own. To do this correctly and efficiently, the teacher should use the 4-Point Critical Writing Rubric.[22] This rubric will ensure that the developed prompt actually produces Critical Writing, as opposed to any other type of writing. To be considered a Critical Writing prompt, the prompt *must* meet all four criteria of the rubric.

4-Point Critical Writing Rubric

1. The BRAIN moves the pencil (nullifies copying, fill in the blank, and similar writing activities).

2. The prompt forces CONNECTION (to almost anything: prior knowledge, another class, a hypothesis, a sibling, etc.).

3. The prompt forces COGNITION (to at least the application level).

4. There is an illusion of accountability (nullifies any writing with limited or no monitoring, such as typical journaling practices).

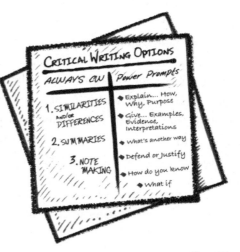

Figure 5.6

Early Primary Critical Writing

Most readers have heard the saying, "A picture is worth a thousand words." For a developing pre-writer, this saying could not be more accurate. While early primary students are in the beginning stages of learning the many varied components of literacy, drawing a

---

[22] Developed by Lead Your School, 2013.

picture allows younger students to unleash their thinking on paper. Drawing a picture provides a pre-writer the opportunity to develop, express, and expand their thinking and ideas. Children, still unprepared to write, can tell a story through their drawing.

Picture writing is one key in learning the writing process. A story begins to unfold as a student talks about the picture. The teacher asks questions or provides simple prompts to open up the conversation. Student thinking is embedded in pictures first, then words follow.

Younger students start to learn how to match words to their pictures. As they become more comfortable with this process, they begin to understand that pictures represent ideas and that ideas can be turned into words on the page. In pre-kindergarten, kindergarten, and early first grade, drawing can be considered Critical Writing when the teacher talks with the student about what their picture means. Helping students to understand that pictures represent ideas and that ideas can be represented first in words and then sentences is a huge concept in early writing and reading.

Younger students are often great critical thinkers. Teachers need to use questions and prompts to expand their thinking even before their formal writing skills develop. Ask students to draw and explain predictions of what happens next in a story that is being read. Have students draw and describe how the main character feels at the beginning of the story and to note changes in their feelings over time. Critical Writing in an early primary math class might include drawing a picture to illustrate what is happening in a story problem. Students might be asked to illustrate and explain what happens when two groups are combined. In science, students could be asked to draw and then explain what they know about water. In any subject or setting, students could dictate to the teacher or draw the most important thing they have learned about a topic at that time. Students could draw a picture of what they already know about a new topic the teacher is just introducing. The possibilities are many, and younger students who express their thinking through drawing and explaining are on their way to becoming good future writers.

Every educator reading this chapter should work to significantly increase the frequency of Critical Writing activities provided in their classroom, on their campus, and in their school district. There is no more powerful instructional tool available to teachers. More Critical Writing produces more successful students and enhances student life opportunities. The effect that daily Critical Writing has on students is amazing. Student content vocabulary will grow. Student thinking skills will blossom. Student complaints about writing and writer's block will begin to evaporate.

With measured and steady progress, the teacher will see consistent growth in deeper student understanding and content mastery. Delivered instruction will improve as the teacher more rapidly determines what their students know and do not know, as revealed through their writing. The only limitations to continued upward growth of student performance would be not enough opportunities to continue to write and a lack of embedded and focused Critical Writing prompts in every lesson.

With that in mind, here is one last suggestion that the authors wish they had learned earlier in their Critical Writing journey. With every Critical Writing prompt created for your students, make sure to write down the "perfect" answer you hope to see as a response. Writing down this perfect answer next to the selected Critical Writing prompt will influence how the lesson is taught, what activities are selected to promote student learning, and how quickly the classroom level of understanding can be informally assessed. Most importantly, looking at the perfect answer you desire will often lead you to edit or clarify your original prompt to make sure it is more likely to elicit exactly what you are expecting to receive from most of your students.

Critical Writing in the Remote Classroom

In remote instructional settings, Critical Writing can often be used in much the same way it is used in a traditional classroom. The execution will differ in that the teacher is not physically present when the students are writing. With the utilization of software that allows teachers to see all students' screens when they are writing (typing), the teacher can effectively be in the Power Zone and has the perfect viewpoint to see who is excelling and who may need additional coaching and support. There are also software and app solutions that allow all students to contribute a quick write in response to a prompt in one electronic location. The use of cloud and web based document sharing systems create a convenient location for students to turn in written assignments for the teacher to review and assess.

The benefit of including Critical Writing in remote instruction is it gives students the opportunity to personalize their learning across the distance of the learning platform. It also provides students with the opportunity to engage in the most powerful learning activity (in terms of impact on student performance) while being taught in a less than optimal learning environment (virtual versus face-to-face instructional settings). Teachers can and should include Critical Writing in both asynchronous and synchronous instructional settings and activities. With asynchronous instruction there is less need for critical quick writes due to the lack of concrete time constraints. However, it is suggested that teachers shy away from the most formal and polished examples of Critical Writing. This is due to the inability of the teacher to provide immediate support and monitoring to students in asynchronous environments. Instead, focus on paragraph length responses to Critical Writing power prompts (see Figure 5.6) or making connections using Venn diagrams and T-charts. With these Critical Writing assignments, the teacher should be more concerned with the quality of student thinking and less concerned with spelling and grammar.

With synchronous lessons, we suggest that teachers leverage the quicker, more informal forms of Critical Writing (see Figure 5.1). Quick responses to Critical Writing power prompts in a chat box, or other virtual collaborative learning space, not only facilitate deeper thinking and retention, but they also allow the teacher to quickly determine the level of student engagement. Additionally, shared access to the entirety of classroom writing also facilitates students making more and faster connections because students are able to read what their peers are writing in real time.

Note making also lends itself to synchronous learning environments. To ensure near universal student participation, the teacher should adopt a standardized note making format (See Figure 5.4) and stop teaching/presenting at regular intervals to provide students with processing and writing time. Before restarting the lesson, have students hold their notes up to the camera so the teacher can quickly scan to see who is participating. For students who are not participating, the teacher should pull them to a small group to address learning and motivational needs once students are released to work on their assignments.

6 WORK IN THE POWER ZONE

Working in the Power Zone is the mortar that connects and strengthens the other fundamental practices. It is the practice that binds, enhances, and completes every other **Fundamental 5** teaching behavior. Throughout this book the Power Zone has been referenced in each of the fundamental practices of good instruction. Effective teachers naturally Close the Lesson in the Power Zone. Effective teachers monitor Frequent, Small Group, Purposeful Talk About the Learning and Critical Writing in the Power Zone. The Power Zone is where effective teachers seize the opportunity to Recognize and Reinforce student academic effort, growth, and success. Think of the Power Zone as the power strip that all the other fundamental practices plug into to make them work. The secret of the Power Zone is to both maximize the time spent working in it and to take advantage of the practice to leverage its effect on the other **Fundamental 5** practices. That is when the power is amplified, and all **The Fundamental 5** practices reach their maximum potential.

It is easy to define the Power Zone, but in the classroom its application is often misunderstood. The Power Zone simply defined is the teacher being in close proximity to students during instruction or monitoring. The Power Zone is where effective teachers spend *more* of their instructional time to ensure learning is occurring. Many teachers and administrators mistakenly believe teachers are expected to spend all their time working in the Power Zone. This is not the case. If one collected a sample of twenty random, short formative classroom observations of a typical teacher over the course of six weeks, that teacher would be observed working in the Power Zone four to twelve times. That is a frequency range of 20% to 60%. This frequency range is neither good nor bad. It is simply typical. For the exceptional teacher in a sample of twenty random classroom observations over the course of six weeks, that teacher would be observed working in the Power Zone twelve to eighteen times. That is a frequency range of 60% to 90%. Not 100%, which frankly is an unreasonable expectation. The exceptional teacher is often observed working in the Power Zone at twice the frequency of their typical peers. The exceptional teacher has figured out, either consciously or subconsciously, that more time in the Power Zone means greater student success in their classroom.

A teacher is working in the Power Zone if they are teaching, demonstrating, lecturing, or monitoring in close proximity to one or more students. When students are engaged in *academic* listening, reading, writing, talking, or assigned work, the teacher is in close proximity teaching, supporting, or monitoring the students. To be effective, the teacher is in the Power Zone *intentionally*. There is an academic purpose to being in the Power Zone that is specific to the instructional activity. The Power Zone is not just a location, it is the teacher's action(s) taking place while the teacher is in the Power Zone that impacts student learning.

The Power Zone with Individuals and Small Groups

The impact of the Power Zone can be leveraged in a variety of configurations—individual students, small groups, and whole group. The key to its effectiveness is driven by teacher actions and engagement while in the Power Zone. When working with individual students and small groups, the teacher is in the Power Zone with the student or group during the instructional moment. During this time in the Power Zone, the teacher may be watching student

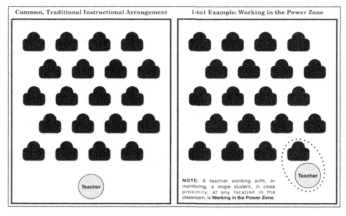

Figure 6.1

practice, reviewing or reteaching a skill, generating conversation, or providing feedback. Being in the Power Zone enhances each of these actions. In most situations the teacher will capitalize on the time with a student or students and then move back into proximity to the other students in the room either by moving on to other students or bringing another group of students into the small group. Skillful teachers can be seen working with a small group, getting up from the small group and taking a lap around the classroom to ensure the

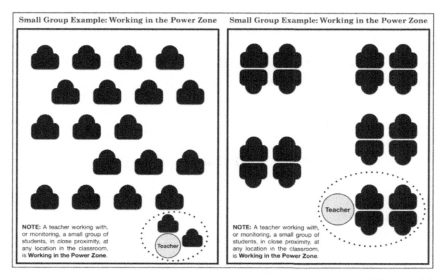

Figure 6.2

other students are continuing their learning, often jotting some quick notes on their progress or Grading on the Fly before returning to the small group. See Figures 6.1 and 6.2.

Location Matters

By working in the Power Zone and moving through the classroom, even when a teacher is lecturing or demonstrating to the whole group, the teacher is better in sync with both individual students and the overall class. This positions the teacher to deliver more student-centric instruction. Effective teachers understand that *location* matters. In fact, where a teacher delivers instruction has a measurable impact on student retention. For example, a teacher delivers the same information to two similar classes. In

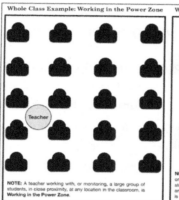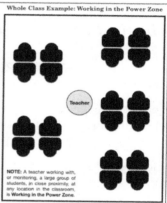

Figure 6.3

the first class, the teacher delivers the information from the front of the room, somewhat removed from students. This would be the traditional lecture position in the classroom. In the second class, the teacher delivers the same information but this time in the Power Zone. When student retention of the information is assessed at some point in the future, students in the second class (the ones who received the information in closer proximity to the teacher) can be expected to perform slightly better. In other words, if the information is important enough for the teacher to share, they should share it in the Power Zone. See Figure 6.3.

As noted previously, a typical teacher is observed working in the Power Zone about 20% to 60% of the time. Typical elementary school teachers cluster towards the top of the range, while typical secondary teachers are represented more often towards the bottom of the range. Again, this is neither good nor bad, just typical. The good news is that this is a measurable improvement from what was typically observed just a decade ago (pre-2010). A decade ago, teachers infrequently moved away from their board or from behind their desk. We know that during the pandemic teachers were purposefully distancing themselves from students, *as even the authors recommended.* However, we are optimistic that post-pandemic Power Zone frequency will rebound.

Why the Power Zone Is Effective

The research on spending time in close proximity to students while teaching or monitoring student work or progress indicates that when a teacher spends more time in the Power Zone, on task behavior increases, retention increases, discipline issues decrease, and the teacher is provided more opportunities to leverage other high-yield instructional practices. A teacher in the Power Zone is better able to engage with their students. Proximity allows a teacher to see what the students are doing, make meaningful comments, and provide targeted support. Working in the Power Zone allows a teacher to manage student practice more effectively because the teacher is right there to see when students are on the right track, support them as needed, and encourage them when they need to give more effort. When students begin to struggle or make critical mistakes, the teacher can give gentle corrections which enhance the student's opportunity for success and reduce frustration. Students are given more timely and specific feedback. The teacher is coming in direct contact with the work the students are doing and can comment immediately with enhanced specificity. Instead of saying, "good job," the teacher knows exactly what the student is working on and what they are doing correctly, and then gives the student timely, specific, individualized feedback, and/or Recognition and Reinforcement. The net result of this is that the more time teachers spend working in the Power Zone, the more that they are able to teach more content, at greater levels of mastery, to more students.

Teachers working in the Power Zone often *micro-adjust* their instruction, making minute adjustments to what they are going to do next, based on what they are seeing in the moment. This is one of the reasons why teachers who work in the Power Zone with greater frequency are generally more effective than teachers who work in the Power Zone with less frequency. The more removed a teacher is from student work, the less likely a teacher will make the timely micro-adjustments that are necessary to support and accelerate student learning. As a teacher begins to spend more time working in the Power Zone, they become more effective and efficient at leveraging what they observe and sense. As with all **The Fundamental 5** practices, the more a teacher uses them, the better they get at using them.

Creating An Effective Power Zone

For a teacher to best leverage and maximize time spent working in the Power Zone, the classroom must be set up for movement. If a room is stuffed with too much furniture, equipment, and materials, then teacher movement is constrained. When this is the case, the odds that the teacher will remain at the front of the room for most of the class increase. Classroom arrangement should allow unobstructed movement by the teacher. Student desks set up in traditional rows generally take up more relative class space than desks arranged in pairs or groups. Classroom technology can also be an impediment to spending more instructional time in the Power Zone. Teachers who are tethered to their desks or smart boards to access instructional technology find it difficult to move into the Power Zone.

Doug Lemov calls this "Breaking the Plane."[23] He describes the plane as the imaginary line that runs across the front of the room. Many teachers are reluctant to move past this imaginary barrier and move out among the students. Teaching in the Power Zone requires moving past that invisible line in the classroom that separates students and teachers and getting teachers in the middle of where the learning is happening.

For a teacher looking to increase the amount of time that they work in the Power Zone, it is recommended that they remove the non-essential furniture, equipment, and materials that impede easy access to the proximity of students at any location in the classroom. This will require a critical look at everything in the room to identify its benefit to immediate student learning and removal of anything that is not significantly adding to current instruction. Student desks should be arranged in a way that both supports student learning and facilitates teacher movement and access to all areas of the classroom. There should be a clear path around the classroom. Make sure that student desks are away from the wall, especially the back wall, allowing the teacher easy movement between students. Additionally, there should be a designated place in the classroom for backpacks and other student possessions to avoid creating a tripping hazard for the teacher moving about the classroom. Teachers need to be able to easily circulate and quickly reach any student that needs support and/or feedback. In overcrowded classrooms this often necessitates minimizing teacher furnishings.

If instructional technology has tethered the teacher to their desk or a particular place in the room, there are solutions. An inexpensive clicker can change slides on a screen, and a wireless keyboard or tablet can allow a teacher to access their computer from anywhere in the classroom. Having students drive the technology allows the teacher to be in the Power Zone as well as give students

---

[23] Lemov, Doug. (2010). *Teach Like a Champion.* New York, NY: Wiley & Sons.

the opportunity to be a part of the instruction. Again, the goal is to better allow a teacher to circulate throughout the room to provide every student with the regular benefit of teacher attention and timely, specific feedback.

Teachers should guard against the passive habit of staying at their desk while a steady stream of students wait in line for their turn to confer with the teacher, have a question answered, or simply be reassured. The proactive replacement practice to adopt is for the teacher to confer with and support students *at the students' desks*. This practice allows the teacher to address the needs of individual students while leveraging the positive effect of teacher proximity to other students in the room. This is the essence of working in the Power Zone.

Grading on the Fly

In the chapter on Recognition and Reinforcement, the concept of Grading on the Fly was introduced. Grading on the Fly is a great way to increase time in the Power Zone with a specific student performance focus and purpose. Teachers who use this strategy leverage proximity and receive real time formative information on student learning. Grading on the Fly makes it easier for the teacher to check on *every* student, even the one student who is trying to disappear in the corner or back of the room. When a teacher is Grading on the Fly, they are looking at student work and giving each student near immediate feedback on the assignment. Teachers do this by making simple, positive grading and editing marks on students' assignments as they are working. These grading and editing marks should mean something to the student and the teacher. Obviously, a checkmark means the answer is correct or the work is on target, motivating the student to keep working with confidence. A plus sign may mean add more details, and a question mark may mean be more specific. However, if an answer is incorrect, the teacher does not mark that with an **X**. Instead, the teacher encourages the student to redo the question, reinforcing the fact that increased or additional effort leads to greater success.

The primary purpose of Grading on the Fly is to give students feedback and allow the teacher to know where the students are in their learning. The ancillary benefits of the practice are two-fold. First, more students complete more work with greater success. This kickstarts a flywheel effect that drives an improvement in overall, long-term class performance. This is especially noticeable when the performance of the classroom where Grading on the Fly is a regularly occurring practice is compared to the performance of a classroom where the teacher does not engage in the practice.

The secondary purpose of Grading on the Fly is to allow the teacher to recapture a tremendous amount of time. Essentially every teacher reviews some student work during a class period, but they leave no record of their review on the assignment. This means that they often review the same work repeatedly, and at the end of the day they "grade" the same work they have already reviewed but left no record. When a teacher Grades on the Fly, they leave a record of their review. At the end of the day, student assignments are not completely graded, but most of them are partially graded. Now all the teacher must do is grade any work that does not have a checkmark. End of class grading time is saved, more individual student support and feedback is provided during class, and student understanding is accelerated and enhanced—win, Win, **WIN**!

Grading on the Fly is one example of purposeful teacher action while working in the Power Zone. Another impactful action is for the teacher to grab a clipboard and begin making notes on individual student progress. Working in the Power Zone allows the teacher to collect real time performance data on students as they work. These teachers create a running formative assessment they use to adjust their instruction and provide students with precise feedback on their growth and overall learning. These running assessment records are generally not recorded as grades but are instead used to assess the quality of instruction and student learning while students are practicing in the classroom.

A final common sense practice for teachers who endeavor to increase the amount of time that they work in the Power Zone is to wear comfortable shoes. In most cases, more time in the Power Zone means more time on your feet. More time on your feet in uncomfortable shoes means foot pain. The more a teacher's feet hurt, the further down the teacher's personal instructional priority list the Power Zone falls.

This does not mean that working in the Power Zone *requires* standing and walking around. The Power Zone is simply proximity instruction and monitoring. In elementary schools, teachers are often observed sitting on the floor with their students or sitting with small groups at a designated small group instruction table. These teachers are working in the Power Zone. Secondary teachers are often observed sitting in their desk chair that they have moved adjacent to a student's desk, engaged in one-to-one or small group instruction. These teachers are also working in the Power Zone. The critical factor is *close proximity*. Teacher location while teaching and monitoring matters...a lot. Maximizing time spent working in the Power Zone validates and amplifies the time, energy, and passion teachers invest in delivering their content. Working in the Power Zone amplifies the effect of each of the other **Fundamental 5** practices, making each more effective and increasing their impact on student learning. Working in the Power Zone is the glue that holds **The Fundamental 5** together.

The Power Zone and Framing the Lesson

Every lesson, every day, should have a Lesson Frame. The primary purpose of the Lesson Frame is to facilitate the closing of the lesson. The Close, when executed appropriately, prompts deeper thinking about the content and serves as proof of lesson understanding and connection. The Close, as evident by its name, should occur in the last two to five minutes of the lesson period.

Working in the Power Zone enhances Lesson Closure because when the teacher is in close proximity to students, student engagement and attention to the Close is enhanced. While students are engaged in the Close, the savvy teacher moves through the Power Zone strategically, positioning themselves near students who are more likely to struggle, purposefully providing motivation and/or support. Because the teacher is in close proximity to students, they can more readily Recognize students with good answers and responses and Reinforce students who are making good attempts and putting forth good effort. In the Power Zone, the teacher can listen to student discussions during a talking Close and read what they are writing during a written Close. The teacher doing so has a very accurate understanding of the outcome of the lesson which positions them to make better instructional decisions as they teach forward. If the Close indicates that most students have mastered the lesson Objective, the class celebrates, and the teacher moves forward at full speed and with full confidence. If the Close indicates that mastery remains elusive, the teacher has a better understanding of what specifically needs to be readdressed and which students need a little more attention and time. Determining this in real time with a high degree of accuracy is only possible if the teacher is working in the Power Zone during the Close. This vital formative information is all but invisible to the teacher who remains distant from students at this critical time.

The Power Zone and Recognition and Reinforcement

The Power Zone could easily and accurately be renamed as the Recognition and Reinforcement Zone. Just as working in the Power Zone enhances the Close, it similarly enhances the effectiveness and impact of Recognition and Reinforcement.

Academic Recognition is the *personal* and *specific* recognition of academic success or growth. Academic Reinforcement is the *personal* and *specific* reinforcement of the effort required to achieve academic success or growth. When the teacher is working in the Power Zone, the personalization and specificity come much more readily. The teacher is right there in the space where the student is, at the moment the success occurs or the effort is expended. All the teacher must do is verbalize what they see. When the teacher is not in the Power Zone, from an observation standpoint, the class becomes more monolithic. The teacher's eyes make it exceedingly difficult to see the tree for the forest.

Recognition and Reinforcement is completely within the control of the teacher. The teacher decides if they are going to implement the practice or not. Proximity to the student makes it much easier to initiate Recognition and Reinforcement. When students are working and the teacher is in close proximity to them, the teacher can observe *individual* student effort and work quality *as it occurs*. It is much easier to talk directly to a student about their work and specifically address effort, persistence, improvement, and/or success as they are working. Also, when the teacher does this, the information is much more relevant and motivating to the student. For example, a teacher observing a student as she works could say the following, "Kandace, I see you have included three really good examples of _____, and you are using one of the strategies we discussed earlier in class. You are headed in a great direction."

Another effective way for teachers to Recognize and Reinforce students while working in the Power Zone is to Grade on the Fly. The practice was discussed in depth earlier. What is germane now is the fact that students who struggle often try to hide in the classroom. These students frequent the back rows, far corners, and inconvenient nooks in the room. When a teacher is Grading on the Fly, no student can hide. The practice helps the teacher seek out every student in the room. This allows the teacher to spend some quality class time with the students who need it most, even when those same students are purposefully trying to avoid the attention.

The Power Zone and Frequent, Small Group, Purposeful Talk About the Learning

Listening to student conversations about the learning can provide the teacher with a wealth of formative information. Students who feel comfortable about the content and can express their thoughts are great resources for students who are struggling with the content. When the teacher is working in the Power Zone during Frequent, Small Group, Purposeful Talk, more students have on-topic conversations, and the teacher is much more aware of student understanding and misunderstanding than the teacher monitoring student conversations outside of the Power Zone.

Without question, Frequent, Small Group, Purposeful Talk has the potential to become messy if a teacher attempts to implement this practice while not in the Power Zone. A teacher opting to leave the Power Zone while students are conversing runs the real risk of losing all the "purposeful" from the session. When the teacher is in the Power Zone during student talk sessions, they are listening for pertinent vocabulary use, prompting some students to extend their thinking, encouraging less confident students to participate in the conversations, and are prepared to end the talk session when students have nothing meaningful left to contribute or begin to get distracted. It is the use of the teacher's *invisible hand* while in the Power Zone that keeps the talk purposeful for most students most of the time.[24]

---

[24] Invisible hand: The unintended, greater group benefit(s) brought about by an individual's practice. A classroom example is when the teacher is working in the Power Zone during a FSGPT session. When this occurs, the student talk is often noticeably more focused and insightful. The individual practice is the teacher in the Power Zone. The greater group benefit is the increase in the number of students having focused and insightful academic conversations. The concept of the invisible hand was first introduced by the economist, Adam Smith, in the book, *The Theory of Moral Sentiments* (1759).

Based on the real time formative information the teacher has mined as students talk, the teacher, often without a conscious decision, makes micro-adjustments to their delivery and activities, making the learning more tailored for the needs of the class. Those same needs are invisible to the teacher who either does not let students talk about the learning or does not monitor in close proximity as students do so.

The Power Zone and Critical Writing

The most powerful of all **The Fundamental 5** practices is Critical Writing. Critical Writing is writing for thinking and connecting. There are no format, length, grammar, or punctuation requirements for Critical Writing. Yes, some Critical Writing has some (or all) of those requirements, but it is not those requirements that make the writing critical. It is the thinking and connecting that occurs that makes the writing critical. Embedding a Critical Writing activity in any lesson makes that lesson more powerful. The hard fact is that the decision not to embed a Critical Writing activity in a lesson is to make that lesson less effective *by design*.

One of the secrets to increasing the amount of Critical Writing in any class is to use the critical quick write. Because a critical quick write is focused and quick, the best way to ensure that thinking and engagement meet the teacher's expectation is for the teacher to be in the Power Zone as students write. Many students initially struggle with and begin to dislike writing because there are too many options to consider before they get started, and there is little initial feedback to let them know they made an appropriate choice and are going in the right direction. By working in the Power Zone, the teacher can provide guidance to the student on how to start for those who are having a difficult time getting going and provide positive or gentle corrective feedback to the students who need a boost of confidence to keep writing.

If students know they are going in the right direction and can correct something quickly, they feel more productive and increase their effort. The more productive they feel, the more they see that their effort pays dividends towards success, and they naturally begin to enjoy writing more...or at least not hate it.

A Cohesive, Interconnected Web of Practice

Essentially, the Power Zone makes all the other **Fundamental 5** practices more effective. It is the mortar between the bricks of the other practices. It seals gaps and spreads the weight evenly, making **The Fundamental 5** a strong, cohesive instructional solution. The Power Zone empowers and provides the teacher with the opportunity to take the pulse of the effectiveness of instruction and the quality of student learning. In the classroom of effective teachers, they are generally observed in the Power Zone as students stop and jot their thoughts before answering a question, they are there when students turn and talk to their partner and share what they are thinking, and again when students respond to the Close in writing. All the while Recognizing and Reinforcing the students throughout the process.

When new teachers, or experienced teachers new to purposeful **Fundamental 5** implementation, attempt these practices it often looks and feels choppy and discrete. That is okay. It is part of the learning curve. Embrace it, get in the Power Zone, and give it your best, over and over. The smoothness will come. The Master Teacher is constantly in the Power Zone transitioning through the other four practices so smoothly it seems subconscious. They can blend **The Fundamental 5** together so seamlessly it is difficult to recognize where one practice stops and the other begins. With purpose and effort, it is within all teachers' reach to join the ranks of the true Master Teacher.

The Power Zone in the Remote Classroom

The more time a teacher spends working in the Power Zone, the more that student on task behavior increases and student discipline issues decrease. Those two factors are the primary focus when considering the Power Zone, or a replacement practice in the remote classroom. Yes, the idea of the Power Zone can be a little tricky in a remote classroom. The whole concept of remote learning separates the teacher from the student, preventing close physical proximity. This is a significant challenge.

It is possible for the teacher to be in close, *relative* proximity to students while they are working thanks to the advances in remote meeting/teaching technology. Many schools have installed software that allows teachers to use their computer to view student work in real time. This gives teachers access to every student's computer and the ability to see student work in the moment.

In a remote classroom when the teacher is engaged in synchronous instruction with all of the students' cameras on, the teacher has the advantage of seeing every student at once or in smaller numbers by changing their screen view. It is also possible to schedule individual and small group student sessions or join breakout rooms. This gives the teacher the opportunity to directly interact with small groups of students and ask key questions that push student learning and inform the teacher on current levels of student understanding.

Any remote delivery practices used by a teacher that increases student on task behavior and decreases either student discipline issues or the number of distracted learners at any given time should be considered a Power Zone replacement practice. There is power in being in close proximity to student learning, even when the students are remote.

7 CONCLUSION

The Innovative School Redesign team was working against the clock to provide options and solutions for fellow practitioners who were doing their level best to meet accountability standards when they noticed the pattern of **The Fundamental 5** reoccurring in exceptional classrooms. The members of the team, especially E. Don Brown, were known within the public school community, and word of their work quickly spread through the school administrator grapevine. With every passing day there were more and more queries of, "What should our teachers do to improve student performance?"

This question led to a 1½ page memo written by the team that essentially said, "We suggest that your teachers use the following five practices as much as possible. They seem to work."

You have made it to this page, so you know that original 1½ page memo has expanded dramatically. You also know why the practices work and how to implement them with increased frequency and quality. Yet the original advice still stands, "Use these practices as much as possible. They ~~seem to~~ work."

Ten years after publishing **The Fundamental 5**, there are thousands of success stories from individual teachers, schools, and school districts that have used **The Fundamental 5** to significantly increase student performance and exceed everyone's expectations. How do we know this? We could point to data and state report cards, but that is not what sticks. What sticks are the teachers, campus leaders, and district leaders that seek us out when we present across the country and share with us how **The Fundamental 5** has changed the trajectory of people's lives: students they taught, staff they worked with, and themselves personally. It is both humbling and overwhelming. To share every success story would be an endless task. Therefore, recognizing the power of brevity, we will share two of these many stories. We selected these stories not because of the unique results but because of how representative the results are.

A typical, hardworking classroom teacher is assigned to teach some of the most at-risk students attending the school and, by extension, enrolled in the district. The pressure to keep student achievement above state mandated performance levels is brutal. The teacher attends and participates in on-going staff development that is provided by the campus. The training is how to implement **The Fundamental 5** at greater frequency and quality. During the training sessions the teacher starts to think, "This makes sense. These are familiar practices. This is practical and doable. What do I have to lose?"

The teacher goes back to the classroom and tells students what to expect. Every day they will know what they are going to learn and what they will do at the end of the class to demonstrate that they learned it. Going forward they can expect to do a lot more talking and writing in the class. Instead of students coming to the teacher's desk, the teacher will go to them. And now, their effort is the most important thing in the class and the teacher will work hard to recognize their effort and improvement so they will know how much it is valued and appreciated.

At first not much changes, but the teacher does not waiver. Slowly, the students figure out the new routines and begin to trust the teacher and engage in the crazy experiment. Individual student performance begins to improve, two points here, three points there. As more students begin to improve, so does overall class performance. By the end of the school year, the teacher, teaching some of the most fragile learners on the campus, has the highest content test scores in the school. By the end of the second year, the teacher has some of the highest test scores in the district. The significantly at-risk students in this teacher's class are now keeping pace with the more advantaged students in the school district. The same teacher, teaching the same type of students, now consistently produces better student performance. Performance that is driven by better teacher practice...a lot of **The Fundamental 5.**

A large urban school is ranked, in terms of student performance, in the bottom 5% of schools in its state. Due to this, the school is facing imminent take over by the state. The school's new principal attends a **Fundamental 5** presentation at a national principal conference. During the presentation the principal begins to think, "This makes sense to me. My staff and I can do this." The principal returns to the campus, gathers the staff, and tells them, "We have one last shot. This is what we're going to do," and then outlines a plan to implement **The Fundamental 5** at high frequency and improved quality.

Two years later, the principal is sitting in the campus conference room talking to the local media about the spectacular improvement in student performance that the campus has made. The campus has moved from the bottom 5% in the state to the top 50%. The media wants to know what secret and magic program the school has adopted. The principal tells the reporters there is no secret program. All teachers are doing is telling the students what they will learn today and how they will demonstrate they got it. Then the students talk and write a lot while their teachers stick close to them to provide support and encouragement as they work. The reporters look at the principal and repeat the question, "What's the magic program?"

There is no magic program. In the stories above, there are hardworking teachers, all manner of students, and a single change...a lot of **The Fundamental 5**. These two examples highlight the near immediate, accessible power of **The Fundamental 5**. These are not new, exotic practices. Teachers are aware of most, if not all, of the individual practices. This is because each practice is a recognized and documented high-yield instructional practice. Even better, essentially every teacher already uses some of the individual practices,

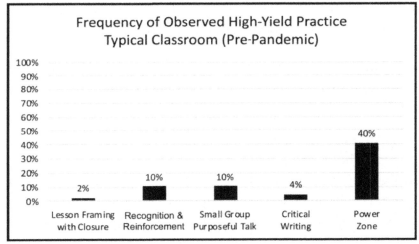

Figure 7.1

occasionally. That is the rub—in most observed classrooms the practices are used...*occasionally*.

Figure 7.1 highlights the patterns seen in a representative sample of observed teachers during a three-to-five-minute formative observation. Each of **The Fundamental 5** practices would be represented, albeit infrequently. The real classroom implication of this limited representation of high-yield instructional practices is unfavorable. Without question, the typical teacher is working hard. But due to the teacher's overreliance on lower-yield instructional practices, student performance results are not commensurate with teacher effort.[25]

It must be noted that there are no realistic expectations that high-yield instructional practices be observed during every classroom visit or that any high-yield practice be observed 100% of the time. A good analogy for a single classroom observation is a single at-bat for a baseball player. During an at-bat, the player may do any number of things, from striking out to hitting a grand slam home run. Regardless of the outcome, that one specific at-bat does not define the player. However, after several at-bats, trends begin to appear: hits, doubles, walks, strike outs, etc. It is these trends that begin to define the player. However, this is where the analogy ends. Every baseball player wants to hit more home runs, but "want to" and ability are not the same thing. Also, there is an opposing pitcher that is doing everything in their power to prevent the hitter from doing the very thing they want to do.

After enough teacher observations, trends in pedagogy begin to appear. The teacher, unlike the hitter, has the capacity to change their practice immediately to alter the observed trends. The teacher can purposefully and consciously improve. As for an opponent, there are times when a student, or students, can be difficult, but rarely are they actively trying to defeat their teacher.

Now consider the exceptional teacher. With enough classroom observations, one notices that the exceptional teacher does not teach dramatically differently from the typical teacher. They teach slightly differently. What they do slightly differently is that they use

---

[25] Less effective instructional practice does *not* mean wrong or bad instructional practice. Less effective simply means that there are other instructional practices that are more effective. It should also be noted that there are times during a lesson where the selection and use of a less effective instructional practice is both appropriate and prudent. Even within the subset of recognized high-yield instructional practices, the practices are not equally effective.

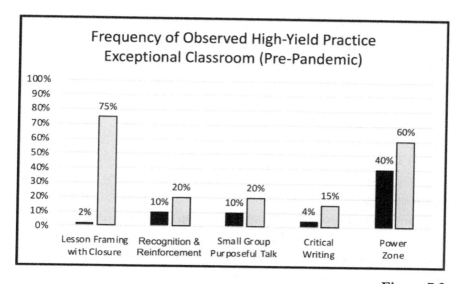

Figure 7.2

certain high-yield instructional practices more often. Figure 7.2 illustrates this.

The black bar graphs represent the typical teacher data shared in Figure 7.1. The gray bar graphs represent the observed frequency of high-yield instructional practices in the classroom of the exceptional teacher. The most dramatic difference in observed practice is with Lesson Framing with Closure. It is the Closure that is the *slightly different* practice, and it explains the magnitude of the differences in the observed frequencies. Typical teachers do not Close their lessons consistently and/or correctly. Exceptional teachers do Close their lessons consistently and correctly. For the remainder of **The Fundamental 5** practices, the increased use of better practice does not seem to be overwhelming until one considers the power of the individual practices that exceptional teachers use more often. For example, with authentic academic Recognition and Reinforcement, the exceptional teacher uses the practice twice as much as the typical teacher. Recognition and Reinforcement is the third most powerful instructional practice which amplifies the overall effect of the differences in implementation. This amplification effect is even more pronounced with Critical Writing. In the exceptional teacher's classroom, it is often observed at three times the frequency of that of the typical teacher. That on its own is significant. Critical Writing represents the most powerful instructional practice, and when that is factored into the equation there is little question why the students in these classrooms excel when compared to their peers in typical classrooms.

The Fundamental 5 is accessible and actionable. Every teacher can use these practices, immediately and more often.[26] The only requirement is for an individual teacher to make the decision to begin and then do so. Would expert training on **The Fundamental 5** be helpful? Yes. Would leadership support in the implementation of **The Fundamental 5** be helpful? Yes. Would attempting to implement **The Fundamental 5** with a partner or partners be helpful? Yes. All of these would be helpful, supportive, and encouraging, but none of them are required. To implement **The Fundamental 5** with greater frequency, which leads to greater quality, all a teacher needs is commitment, a plan, and a dash of perseverance. The commitment is up to the reader. We can provide the plan. Then just stick with it.

---

[26] There are some settings, courses, grade levels, and/or students where all five practices of **The Fundamental 5** are not applicable, practical, or appropriate. When this is the case, the teacher simply implements the practices that are appropriate for the situation with even greater frequency. For example, the exceptional early primary teacher is observed working in the Power Zone with greater frequency than the exceptional secondary teacher but uses Critical Writing less often. The exceptional performance class teacher can be expected to use Critical Writing significantly less often than the exceptional academic content teacher. But their use of Recognition and Reinforcement is often much higher. Bottom line, if one or more of **The Fundamental 5** practices are not a practical, workable option, overcompensate with the remaining practices that are appropriate.

How to Become an Exceptional Teacher in 7 Easy Steps

Academic Courses: Grades K-2

1. Frame every lesson and Close every lesson. Close the Lesson with either a similarity/difference prompt or a summarization prompt. A talking Close is most common and always appropriate. Use a written Close when possible and appropriate.
2. Build and maintain a culture of academic talk. Constantly remind students that talking about content and the assigned classwork is always appropriate. Encourage students to assist any of their peers that ask for help or clarification, especially if you, the teacher, are not immediately available or accessible.
3. Embed a Frequent, Small Group, Purposeful Talk session at each transition point in the lesson. The flow of the typical lesson should be as follows: direct instruction, FSGPT, guided practice, FSGPT, group or individual practice.
4. Embed age appropriate Critical Writing activities as frequently as possible.
5. Live in the Power Zone.
6. Constantly Reinforce student effort and Recognize student improvement. Grade on the Fly as much as possible.
7. Don't quit.

Academic Courses: Grades 3 and Higher

1. Frame every lesson and Close every lesson. Close the Lesson with either a similarity/difference prompt or a summarization prompt. Use a written Close at least three times a week.

2. Build and maintain a culture of academic talk. Constantly remind students that talking about content and the assigned classwork is always appropriate. Encourage students to assist any of their peers that ask for help or clarification, especially if you, the teacher, are not immediately available or accessible.
3. Embed a Frequent, Small Group, Purposeful Talk session at each transition point in the lesson. The flow of the typical lesson should be as follows: direct instruction, FSGPT, guided practice, FSGPT, group or individual practice.
4. Teach students how to use a quick and easy note making template (see Figure 5.5). Set and maintain the expectation that students will engage in note making when:
    a. The teacher is presenting or demonstrating.
    b. Students are reading or watching something.
    c. When a good point is made during an academic conversation.
    d. When the student figures out something critical, useful, or important and wants/needs to remember it.
    e. It is often appropriate and effective to have transition FSGPT sessions where students compare and share their notes.
5. Live in the Power Zone.
6. Constantly Reinforce student effort and Recognize student improvement. Grade on the Fly as much as possible.
7. Don't quit.

Performance Courses

1. Frame every lesson and Close every lesson. Close the Lesson with either a similarity/difference prompt, a

summarization prompt, a connection prompt, a reflection prompt, or an evaluation prompt.[27] Use a written Close if appropriate, possible, and *practical*.

2. Build and maintain a culture of academic talk. Constantly remind students that talking about content and the assigned classwork is always appropriate. Encourage students to assist any of their peers that ask for help or clarification, especially if you, the teacher, are not immediately available or accessible.

3. Embed a Frequent, Small Group, Purposeful Talk session at each transition point in the lesson. The flow of the typical lesson should be as follows: direct instruction, FSGPT, guided practice, FSGPT, group or individual practice.

4. Live in the Power Zone.

5. Constantly Reinforce student effort and Recognize student improvement.

6. If any of **The Fundamental 5** practices are not appropriate, possible, or practical for the setting or course, then increase the use of **The Fundamental 5** practices that are.

7. Don't quit.

---

[27] Examples of connection, reflection, and evaluation prompts include but are not limited to: list, give examples, why, explain, justify, how do you know, and what if. In performance courses students are often engaged in applying level cognition activities and/or the individual component skills of a more complicated process. The additional Closing prompts options can be used to facilitate deeper thinking about or more nuanced understandings of the performance.

Welcome to the Big Show...Or How to Let Observers Know That You are an Exceptional Teacher

The Set-up

1. Always have the Lesson Frame posted prominently on the white board.
2. Live in the Power Zone. Lecture from the Power Zone. Monitor students from the Power Zone. Make every trip out of the Power Zone as brief as possible.

When Any Observer Enters the Classroom

3. Ignore the observer. You are busy teaching content or monitoring student work. Instead consider the activity currently in play. Based on the activity do the following:

   a. *If you are lecturing or demonstrating...*
      i. At the next natural break point, stop talking or demonstrating. Say, "Class, I've been talking for a while, now it is your turn. Based on the information I've been sharing, talk with your partner about the most important things to remember so far. You have one minute. Go."
      ii. Move through the classroom and monitor student conversations.
      iii. After one minute say, "Okay class, back to me. I heard some really good discussions about what is important to remember. Before we get started again, let's take 45 seconds and jot down those important things so we can use them when we get to the assignment."

      iv. Move through the classroom and monitor students as they jot down their notes.

      v. Draw a big checkmark or a happy face on the note pages of students who are working diligently and/or have written down good points.

b. *If the students are working on an assignment...*

      i. Get the class' attention and say, "I'm seeing a lot of hard work and great effort right now. Let's do a quick check to see if we are all on the right track. Share with your partner the strategies you are using to get the correct answer. If your partner is confused, help them overcome that confusion. You have one minute. Go."

      ii. Move through the classroom and monitor student conversations.

      iii. After one minute say, "Okay class, back to me. I heard some really good discussions about the strategies that are being used on this assignment. Before we get started again, let's take 45 seconds and jot down the things we need to remember as we complete this work."

      iv. Move through the classroom and monitor students as they jot down their notes.

      v. Draw a big checkmark or a happy face on the note pages of students who are working diligently and/or have written down good points.

c. *If the class is engaged in a FSGPT session...*

    i. As the session concludes, say, "Okay class, back to me. I heard some really good discussions about (the topic). Before we get started again, let's take 45 seconds and jot down the really important things we discussed so we don't forget them."

    ii. Move through the classroom and monitor students as they jot down their notes.

    iii. Draw a big checkmark or a happy face on the note pages of students who are working diligently and/or have written down good points.

d. *If the students are engaged in a Critical Writing activity...*

    i. Get the class' attention and say, "I see a lot of effort and deep thinking right now. Let's do a quick check to see if our writing is on the right track. Share with your partner the idea(s) you are attempting to communicate and what points you are making or will make to support those ideas. You have two minutes. Go."

    ii. Move through the classroom and monitor student conversations.

    iii. After two minutes say, "Okay class, back to me. I heard some really good discussions about your writing. Keep those discussions in mind as you continue the assignment."

    iv. Move through the classroom and monitor students as they recommence writing.

    v. Draw a big checkmark or a happy face on the pages of students who are working diligently and/or are producing quality writing.

    e. *If nothing instructional is occurring in the classroom...*
        i. This will never happen.
        ii. You are an exceptional teacher.

4. While informally grading the students' writing on the fly, look at the observer and give them a big wink. The observer has now witnessed the seamless implementation of all five of **The Fundamental 5** practices as a cohesive unit.

The teacher who can do what is described above demonstrates and communicates that the implementation of **The Fundamental 5** is such a regular and natural occurrence in the classroom that it can be used both anytime and all the time. For those who might consider doing the above for the benefit of an observer as a dog and pony show, we respond, *"So what?"* Yes, the immediate and cued change in teacher practice and slight deviation in class activity might be done to impress an observer, but the change and the deviation immediately benefits every student in the classroom. The effect being similar to an instructional vitamin booster shot. Due to the slight, cued changes in teacher practice, student engagement and thinking are enhanced, stronger connections to the content are made, and students are better positioned to successfully complete their assigned classwork. This occurs while the students are blissfully unaware of what is occurring at the professional and adult level.

The Fundamental 5 implemented with greater frequency and greater quality significantly upgrades teacher practice. This upgrade in teacher practice has a positive, measurable impact on student performance. As the authors noted and recommended over a decade ago, teachers should implement **The Fundamental 5** as a cohesive unit. It works. We conclude with the wisdom shared by a

Fundamental 5 pioneer. When asked what she attributed the exceptional performance of her students to, she replied with one direct sentence: *"Don't second guess yourself, just* **Fundamental 5** *the heck out of every lesson."*

ABOUT THE AUTHORS

Sean Cain and Mike Laird are the authors of:

- *The Fundamental 5: The Formula for Quality Instruction*
- *The Classroom Playbook: The Power of a Common Scope and Sequence*
- *The Reboot: School Operations in an Unpredictable World*
- *The Reboot Classroom: Teacher Decisions in the Time of COVID-19*

Sean Cain spent the formative years of his career working in difficult instructional settings. Recognized for the success of his students and the systems he designed and implemented, he quickly progressed through the instructional leadership ranks. This culminated in his last public education position as State Director of Innovative School Redesign (Texas). Currently, Cain serves as the

Chief Idea Officer for Lead Your School (LYS), a confederation of successful school leaders dedicated to improving student, campus, and district performance. A passionate speaker, Cain is a sought after national presenter and trains educators in school districts across the country. The co-author of the best-selling book *The Fundamental 5: The Formula for Quality Instruction*, he is known for his ability to make complex problems solvable and transform theory into actionable practice.

Mike Laird is a retired assistant superintendent, adjunct professor, and U.S. Army Reserve Major. The co-author of the best-selling book *The Fundamental 5: The Formula for Quality Instruction*, his work continues on campuses across the country supporting teachers and mentoring school leaders. A respected national presenter, Laird combines his school and military leadership experience to prepare today's educator to succeed in the modern high stakes school accountability environment.

Sherilynn Cotten has been a recognized educator for over 40 years, successfully serving as a teacher, principal, instructional expert, and school improvement consultant. Cotten established her reputation as a nationally awarded math teacher, author, and presenter. As a campus leader she was known for improving student performance in even the most challenging of instructional settings.

Currently, Cotten works as a school improvement consultant combining her expertise in curriculum and instruction, data analysis, and instructional leadership, with her practical implementation ideas to coach teachers, campus administrators, and central office school leaders as they work to improve student outcomes.

Jayne Ellspermann is an accomplished educator and school leader who spent 25 years as an elementary, middle, and high school principal, culminating with the dual honors of being named the National Association of Secondary School Principals (NASSP) National Principal of the Year and then being elected to serve as NASSP's President. Ellspermann now works with schools and school districts throughout the country to support improving student performance through high-yield instructional practices and intentional leadership.